TURKEY

• AT COST •

A TRAVELLER'S GUIDE

Fay Smith

LITTLE HILLS PRESS

ACKNOWLEDGEMENTS

We are most grateful to the Office of the Consulate-General of the Turkish Republic in Sydney for their assistance in the preparation of this book and for the use of the photographs. A special thanks goes to Mr. Avni Karsloglu from the Consulate and Mr. Yekta Gokyildirim of Trans Turk Travel.

Cover photograph by Mark Butler

© Photographs-Turkish Ministry of Tourism and Information
© Text-Little Hills Press, 1988

Typeset by Midland Typesetters, Victoria
Printed in Australia by Globe Press Pty. Ltd.
Production by Vantage Graphics

Little Hills Press Pty. Ltd.,
Tavistock House, 34 Bromham Road,
Bedford MK40 2QD
United Kingdom

Regent House, 37-43 Alexander St.,
Crows Nest. NSW, 2065. Australia

ISBN 0 949773 76 X

DISCLAIMER
Whilst all care has been taken by the publisher and author to ensure that the information is accurate and up to date, the publisher does not take responsiblity for the information published herein. The recommendations are those of the author, and as things get better or worse, places close and others open up some elements in the book may be inaccurate when you get there. Please write and tell us about it so we can update in subsequent editions.

CONTENTS

TURKEY IN BRIEF

Turkey's land mass is 780,000 sq. km. with 97% in Asia (the Anatolian plateau) and 3% in Europe (Thrace). The European and Asian sides are divided by the Bosphorus, the Sea of Marmara and the Dardanelles.

Turkey is the birthplace of many ancient civilisations including the Hittites, Byzantines and Ottomans, remains of which can still be seen throughout the country. It is synonymous with antiquity–Homer wrote of Troy, St. Paul lived and wrote in Ephesus, Anthony gave part of Turkey to Cleopatra as a wedding present and the Virgin Mary spent her last days near Izmir. St. Nicholas (Santa Claus) lived in Derme, Noah's Ark came to rest on Mount Ararat, the Tigris and Euphrates still flow in eastern Turkey, and Bursa was the first capital of the Ottoman Empire which stretched to Vienna and throughout North Africa.

In more recent times, Anzac and British troops fought the Turks at Gelibolu (Gallipoli) and the victor, Kemal Ataturk founded the present Republic of Turkey in Ankara.

Turkey is rich in handicrafts, magnificent oriental carpets, beautiful pottery, leathergoods, jewellery and copperware and Turkish food ranks with French and Chinese as one of the three major cuisines of the world.

POPULATION

Turkey has a population of 51,000,000 half of whom live in the countryside. The major cities are Istanbul (5,500,000), Ankara, the capital (2,500,000), Izmir (1,500,000), Adana (776,000) and Bursa (650,000).

RELIGION

99% of the population are Moslem, but Turkey is a secular state which guarantees freedom of worship to non-Moslems.

Five times a day the Muezzin (priest) calls the faithful to prayer in the mosque. Before entering a mosque Moslems wash themselves and remove their shoes. Foreign visitors should also remove their shoes and show the respect they would in any other house of worship, avoiding visiting the mosque during prayer time. Women should cover their heads and arms and not wear

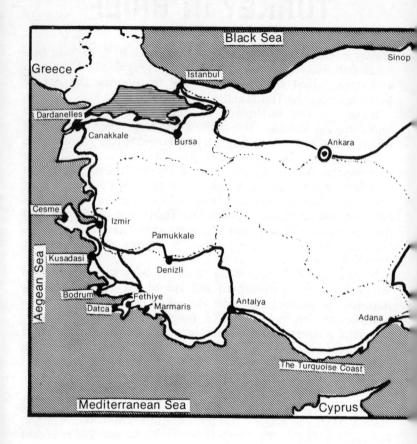

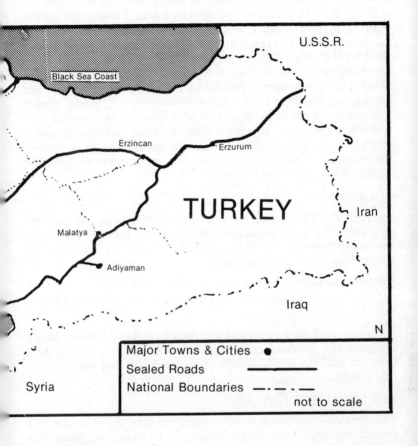

miniskirts. Men should not wear shorts. In certain famous mosques overalls are provided for those not suitably dressed.

There are two religious holidays in Islam. Firstly, the 3 days Seker Bayrami (Candy Festival), when sweets are eaten to celebrate the end of the fast of Ramazan. Secondly, the 4 days Kurban Bayrami (Festival of Sacrifices) when sacrificial sheep are slaughtered and their meat distributed to the poor. The dates of these festivals change according to the Moslem calendar, and during the festivals shops and government offices are closed.

Ramazan is the Islamic month of fasting. In this period even tourists are expected to refrain from smoking, eating or drinking alcohol in the period from sunrise to sunset. In East Turkey, Ramazan is adhered to faithfully, not so however in Istanbul or the other tourist centres.

ECONOMY

Agriculture: This plays a very important role in the Turkish economy. The main crops are wheat, cotton, tobacco and fruit. Sheep are Turkey's most important livestock, and Turkey is the major European wool producer.

Natural resources: The principal minerals extracted are coal, chrome (an important export), iron, copper, bauxite, sulphur and oil.

Industry: Industry is developing rapidly and is directed mainly towards the processing of agricultural product, metallurgy, textiles, and the manufacture of automobiles and agricultural machinery.

POLITICAL STRUCTURE

The Turkish Republic is a democracy. The rule of law exists. The Grand National Assembly is elected by universal suffrage. The executive power is exercised by the President of the Republic and the Council of Ministers. Turkey is a member of NATO, OECD, and the Council of Europe and is an associate member of the EEC.

LANGUAGE

The Turkish language is neither Indo-European nor Semitic, but belongs to the Ural-Altaic group and has an affinity to the Finno-Hungarian language. Turkish is written with Latin characters and is spoken by some 150,000,000 people in the world, thanks to the efforts of Ataturk.

Following are a few letters which have special pronunciations—

c	=	j
ç	=	ch

ğ (soft g-unpronounced but serves to extend the preceding vowel)

i (undotted i)	=	between i and e
ö	=	oe
s	=	sh
ü	=	as in French 'tu'
Cami (mosque)	=	Jami
Foça	=	Focha
Dag (mountain)	=	Daa
Topkapi	=	Topkapeu
Göreme	=	Goereme
Kuşadasi	=	Kushadaseu
Ürgüp	=	Urgup

Everyday Phrases and Polite expressions

To the words 'hos geldiniz' (welcome) you reply 'hos bulduk'.

Hello	Merhaba
Goodbye	Allahaismarlakid (said by the person leaving)
	Gule gule (said by the person seeing someone off)
Good morning	Gunaydin
Good evening	Iyi aksamlar
Good night	Iyi aksamlar
How are you	Nasilsiniz?
I am well thank you	Iyiyim, tesekkur ederim
Please	Lutfen
Thank you	Tesekkur ederim, or mersi
Yes	Evet
No	Hayir
There is	Var
There is not	Yok (used to express the availability or unavailability of something respectively)

Numbers

1	Bir	3	Uc	5	Bes
2	Iki	4	Dort	6	Alti

7	Yedi	40	Kirk	101	Yuz bir
8	Sekiz	50	Elli	200	Iki yuz
9	Dokuz	60	Altmis	300	Uc yuz
10	On	70	Yetmis	1000	Bin
11	On bir	80	Seksen	2000	Iki bin
25	Yirmibes	90	Doksan		
30	Otuz	100	Yuz		

The time

When	Ne zaman
Yesterday/today	Dun, bugun
Tomorrow	Yarin
Morning/afternoon	Sabah, ogleden sonra
Evening/night	Aksam, gece
One hour	Bir saat
What is the time?	Saat kac?
At what time	Saat kacta?

The days

Sunday	Pazar
Monday	Pazartesi
Tuesday	Sali
Wednesday	Carsamba
Thursday	Persembe
Friday	Cuma
Saturday	Cumartesi

While travelling

Airport	Hava alani
Port	Liman
Town centre	Sehir merkezi
Where is it?	Nerede?
Is it far?	Uzak mi?
Tourism bureau	Turizm burosu
Repair garage	Bir tamirci
A good hotel	Iyi bir otel
A restaurant	Bir lokanta
Attention	Dikkat

In the hotel

A room	Bir oda
Two people	Iki kisi
A room with bath	Banyolu bir oda

What is the price?	Fiati nedir
Hot water	Sicak su
A supplementary bed	Ilave bir yatak
Breakfast	Kahvalti
Butter	Tereyag
Coffee	Kahve
Tea	Cay
Milk	Sut
Sugar	Seker
The bill	Hesap

In the garage

Petrol	Benzin
Petrol station	Benzin istasyonu
Oil	Motor yagi
Change of oil	yag degistirme
Tyre	Lastik
Brakes	Frenier
Spark Plugs	Bujiler
It does not work	calismiyor

Shopping

How much is it?	Bu ne kadar?
It is very expensive	Cok pahali
I do not like it	Begenmedim
Is it old?	Eski mi?
Gold	Altin
Silver	Gumus
Leather	Deri
Copper	Bakir

In the restaurant

Bread	Ekmek
Water	Su
Mineral Water	Maden suyu
Fruit juice	Meyva suyu
Wine	Sarap
Beer	Bira
Ice	Buz
Meat	Et
Mutton	Koyun eti
Lamb	Kuzu eti

Beef	Sigir eti
Veal	Dana eti
Chicken	Pilic
Fish	Balik

MONETARY SYSTEM

The national monetary unit is the Turkish Lira (TL). The coinage is in 5, 10, 25 and 50 lira pieces. Bank notes are of 10, 20, 50, 100, 500, 1,000, 5,000 and 10,000 lira. The exchange rates for foreign currencies are published daily.

Roughly they are —

US$	=	842 TL
A$	=	615 TL
NZ$	=	501 TL
CAN$	=	683 TL
£	=	1402 TL

Eurocheques can be cashed immediately, as can traveller's cheques upon producing identification. However it may take ages to cash cheques from private accounts because the relevant bank abroad has to be contacted. So forget your personal cheque book.

POSTAL SYSTEM

Turkish post offices are easily recognisable by their yellow PTT signs. Major post offices are open 8.00 a.m.- 12 midnight Monday-Saturday and 9.00 a.m.-7.00 p.m. Sunday. These are found only in the tourist centres of Istanbul, Ankara, etc. Small post offices have the same opening hours as government offices.

Postal charges vary between US$0.25 and US$0.50.

Poste restante letters should be addressed 'poste restant' to the central post office 'Merkez Postanesi' in the town of your choice. It is only necessary to produce an identification card when collecting your letter.

PHONE CALLS

Within a city–40.00 TL is paid at a post office in return for a token, which is slotted into the machine as soon as the required number answers.

Inter-city–for all such calls, except the major cities and tourist centres which are direct dial, it is necessary to request the call at a post office. Calls can be made normal, urgent (acele) or very urgent (yildirim).

International-same as inter-city.

OPENING TIMES

Government Offices-8.30 a.m.-12.30 p.m. 1.30-5.30 p.m. (Monday-Friday)
Banks 8.30 a.m.-12 noon 1.30-5.00 p.m. (Monday-Friday)
Shops 9.00 a.m.- 1.00 p.m. 2.00-7.00 p.m. (Monday-Saturday)

Summer hours: In the Aegean and Mediterranean regions of Turkey government offices and many other establishments are closed during the afternoon during the summer months. These summer hours are fixed each year by the province governors. Check with your travel agent or the hotel when you get to Turkey.

EMBASSIES AND CONSULATES

Ankara (Embassies)	United States-Ataturk Bulvan 110, Tel. 26 54 70 Australian-Nenehatun Cad. 83, Gaziosmanpasa, Tel. 39 27 50-51 British-Sehit Ersan Cad. 46/A, Cankaya, Tel. 27 43 10 Canadian-Nenehatun Cad. 75, Gaziosmanpasa, Tel. 27 58 03 There is no resident New Zealand representative in Turkey. Embassies in Athens or Rome should be contacted.
Istanbul (Consulates)	United States-Mesrutiyet Cad. 104, Tel. 14 36 200-09 British-Tepebasi, Mesrutiyet Cad. 34, Tel. 14 47 540
Izmir (Consulates)	United States-Ataturk Cad. 386, Tel. 13 21 35 British-Necatibey Bulvari 19/4, Tel. 14 54 70-9

MISCELLANEOUS

Local Time: G.M.T. + 3 hours (winter)
      G.M.T. + 2 hours (summer)

Electricity: 220 volts AC all over Turkey. The voltage is clearly marked on all hotel power points.

Tap water: Official brochures state that it is safe to drink in all cities as it is heavily chlorinated. Judge for yourself. Some areas are okay–others, especially in the outlying areas, are suspect.

Weights and Measures: Metric system. For U.S. citizens some equivalents –

A litre (l.) is slightly more than a US quart.
A kilogram (kg.) is 2.2 pounds.
A metre (m.) is 39 inches.
A kilometre (km.) is 5/8 of a mile.

Foreign newspapers: Available at the embassies and first class hotels in large cities the day after printing.
   The Ankara 'Daily News', an English language daily is sold in most Turkish cities which tourists visit.

Interpreter-guides: Ministry of Culture and Tourism bureaux and some travel agents can provide professional interpreter-guides. Travel agents are obliged to provide professional guides on all of their tours. Since Ani lies in a military zone, it is necessary to obtain a special permission from the Local Security Authority in Kars before being allowed to visit the ruins.

Doctors and Dentists: A great number of Turkish doctors and dentists speak a foreign language, and many of them have received training abroad. Such doctors and dentists can be found in Turkey's major hospitals, and in addition their are certain foreign operated hospitals in Instanbul. Check with the receptionist at your hotel.

TRAVEL GUIDELINES

HOW TO GET TO TURKEY

BY AIR

Turkish Airlines (THY) has regular flights in Boeing 707s, 727s, DC9s Airbus, DC10s and F28s for Ankara, Istanbul, Izmir, Antalya and Dalaman from the principal capitals and the important cities of the world.

International Airlines—

British Airways has daily flights from the U.K. to Istanbul.
Singapore Airlines has flights from Sydney and Singapore to Istanbul.
Pan American has daily flights from New York to Istanbul.
Lufthansa has daily flights from Germany to Istanbul and Ankara, and less frequent services to Antalya and Izmir.

BY SEA

Passenger Ferries: Turkish Maritime Lines have regular services to Turkish ports from Ancona (Italy) and Magosa (Northern Cyprus). Apart from the numerous cruises in the Mediterranean, several shipping companies have regular services to the ports of Istanbul, Izmir and Kusadasi.

Car-Ferries: The Turkish Maritime Lines' car-ferry sails on the Ancona-Izmir-Ancona line every week from the end of May to the end of September.

Maritime Lines between Turkey and Greece

Cesme–Chios (ferry boats)
Three services a week from 1st June to 15th July; one service daily from 16th July to 1st September. Crossing: 1 hour. Price US$15.00 (adults), US$7.50 (children), US$75.00 (vehicles from 750-1250 kg), US$90.00 (vehicles from 1250-1500 kg).

Kusadasi–Samos (boats and speed boats)
Several daily services starting from 1st May. Crossing: 2 hours (boat). Price: US$25.00 per person (boat) return ticket US$30.00 (same day). Most of the boats can take only one or two cars, price US$50.00 (up to 1000 kg). US$55.00 (up to 1500 kg), US$60.00 (1500 kg and over).

11

Bodrum–Cos (boat)
Every day except Sunday. Crossing: 1 hour 30 minutes. Price: US$15.00 per person.

Marmaris–Rhodes (boats and ferry boats)
Services every day both directions except Sunday. Crossing: 3 hours 30 minutes. Price: US$15.00 per person.

BY RAIL
From Europe by the Orient Express.

BY ROAD

By private car: London–Istanbul approximately 3000 km. Route: Calais or Ostend to Brussels, Cologne and Frankfurt; from Frankfurt there are two alternative routes –
1. Nuremberg, Linz, Vienna, Budapest, Belgrade, or
2. Stuttgart, Munich, Salzburg, Ljubliana, Zagreb, Belgrade, then to Nis, Sofia, Edirne and Istanbul.
One can also use the car ferry from Venice or Ancona by driving south from Munich to Venice rather than going on to Salzburg.

By coach: There are regular services between Turkey and Austria, France, Germany and Switzerland, also Iraq, Iran, Jordan, Saudi Arabia, Kuwait and Syria.

STUDENT REDUCTIONS
Some Turkish organisations, such as Turkish Airlines, recognise the ISTC card and accordingly grant reductions to holders of these cards. The price reductions offered to students are as follows:

Turkish Airlines–International flights–60%; Domestic flights–10%.
Turkish Maritime Lines–International line–15% single; 25% return. Domestic lines–50%.
Railways–10%.
Cinemas and concerts–50%.

WHEN TO GO
Marmara, Aegean and Mediterranean Coasts: Typical Mediterranean climate with hot summers and mild winters. The swimming season becomes shorter the further north one goes.
Marmara and North Aegean–June to September.
South Aegean and Mediterranean–April to October.
Black Sea coasts: Temperate climate with warm summers, mild

Istanbul, Looking towards the Suleymaniye Mosque

Istanbul, Bosphorus Bridge

St. Sophia

winters and a relatively high rainfall. Swimming season: June to September.

Central and Eastern Anatolia: Steppe climate with hot dry summers (not torrid) and cold winters. Even in summer, the nights are cool.

Average temperatures- Celsius(Fahrenheit)	Jan	April	July	Oct.
Marmara region (Istanbul)	7(44)	16(63)	28(82)	19(66)
Aegean region (Izmir)	9(48)	20(68)	30(86)	21(70)
Mediterranean (Antalva)	11(52)	22(72)	32(90)	23(73)
Black Sea region (Trabzon)	8(46)	16(63)	27(81)	18(64)
Central Anatolia (Ankara)	4(39)	15(59)	30(86)	18(64)
Eastern Anatolia (Erzurum)	−9(16)	6(43)	20(68)	12(54)

PASSPORTS AND VISAS

A valid passport is required, without visa, for stays of up to three months. No vaccinations are necessary.

CURRENCY REGULATIONS

Limits: There is no limit on the amount of foreign currency that may be brought into Turkey, but not more than US$1000 worth of Turkish currency may be brought into or taken out of the country.

Exchange slips: The exchange slips for the conversion of foreign currency into Turkish Lira should be kept, since you will be required to show these when reconverting your Turkish lira back into foreign currency, and when taking souvenirs out of the country (to prove that they have been purchased with legally exchanged foreign currency).

CUSTOMS REGULATIONS

On entry

You can import 400 cigarettes, 50 cigars, 200 gr. tobacco, 1 kg. coffee, 1.5 kg. instant coffee, 1 kg. tea and 5 (100 cc) or 7 (70cc) bottles of spirit of which no more than three shall be of the same brand.

Drugs–Be sensible. If you smoke pot, indulge in heroin, cocaine, etc. then forget Turkey. We suggest you look at the movie 'Midnight Express' before you come. Penalties are harsh in this country for possession.

On Exit

Concerning gifts and souvenirs, for a new carpet a proof of purchase, and for old items a certificate from a directorate of a museum is necessary.

The export of antiques from Turkey is forbidden.

FORMALTIES FOR MOTORISTS

Vehicles and towed sea craft can be taken into Turkey for up to three months without a Carnet de Passage. The vehicle is simply registered in the owner's passport and this registration is cancelled when the owner leaves the country. If a tourist wishes to visit another country from Turkey without his car he should take the car to the nearest Customs Authority so that the registration of the car in his passport may be cancelled. Drivers need a three-sectioned driving licence, or an international driving licence.

A motorist should have either–

1. Green Card International Insurance, endorsed for Turkish territory both in Europe and Asia, or

2. Turkish third party insurance, which can be obtained from any of the insurance agencies at the frontier posts.

Petrol prices are below most European countries, although there are slight variations depending on the nearness of a filling station to a refinery. Some examples of prices per litre are as follows.

Regular–US$0.47 Super–US$0.50 Diesel–US$0.33

The brands of petrol available are: Petrol Ofisi, Turk Petrol, B.P., Mobil and Shell. 'Super' grades of petrol can be found all over the country save in the most isolated parts. Filling stations are well distributed over all roads, and those on the main highways often have attached service stations and restaurants and are open for fairly long hours. It depends on the route..

Traffic drives on the right and the Turkish highway code is similar to those of european countries. Outside the cities traffic moves very freely, the Istanbul-Ankara highway being the only one on which traffic is heavy. There is a 50 kph speed limit in urban centres and a 99 kph limit outside urban centres, and it is best to avoid night driving.

HOW TO TRAVEL IN TURKEY

BY AIR

Turkish Airlines (THY) provides an important network of interior flights from the international airports of Istanbul, Ankara and Izmir to all of the major Turkish cities.

There are regular bus connections from airport to air terminal, for Istanbul, Ankara, Izmir and all other airports.

Reductions: 5% on return tickets; 10% for students and married couples; 20% for sports groups of 10 or more; 90% discount for children under 2 if no seat is occupied; 50% for children from 2-12.

BY SEA

The Turkish Maritime Lines have several coastal services providing excellent opportunities for sightseeing. All these services depart from the Eminonu or Karakoy sides, or Istanbul's Galata Bridge, and it is advisable to make early reservations for tourist cruises.

Istanbul services–

(a) Bogazi (Bosphorus) car ferry: Kabatas (European side)–Uskudar (Asian side), departing from both sides every 15 minutes crossing in 15 minutes.
(b) Bogazi tour: Departing from Eminonu and zig-zagging up the Bosphorus to Anadolu Kavagi.
(c) Princes Island service: Eminonu-Buyukada (largest of islands), crossing in 1 hour 30 minutes.

Marmara car ferries–

Kartal (20 km outside Istanbul on the Asian side)–Yalova (south coast of Marmara) crossing from both sides frequently in 1 hour 40 minutes, Istanbul-Mudanya-Gemlik and Istanbul-Bandirma: one service per week.

Canakkale Bogazi (Dardanelles) ferries: Gelibolu (European side)–Lapseki (Asian side): crossing once every two hours from each side, and Eceabat (European side)–Canakkale (Asian side) crossing once every two hours from each side in 30 minutes.

Marmara Sea Services

Istanbul–Mudanya: all year Friday, depart Istanbul 9.00 a.m. In summer Sunday also, depart 9.00 a.m.

Istanbul–Avsa: Every day in July and August, depart Istanbul 8.30 a.m., extra service Friday departs Istanbul 5.30 p.m.

Istanbul–Bandirma: all year, every day, depart Istanbul 8.30 a.m.

Istanbul–Karabiga: (via Saraylar Koyu, Marmara, Avsa)–every Wednesday with Saturday service in summer, depart 9.30 a.m.

Istanbul–Gemlik: all year Friday, with Sunday service in summer, depart Istanbul 9.00 a.m.

Mediterranean Cruise

Istanbul–Alanya–Istanbul line: A 10 day cruise with stops in Izmir, Kusadasi, Gulluk, Bodrum, Datca, Marmaris, Fethiye, Antalya and Alanya. One service a week in summer, departs from Istanbul on Wednesday at 2.00 p.m.

Black Sea Cruise

Istanbul–Trabzon–Istanbul line: a 6 day cruise operating weekly stopping in Sinop, Samsun, Giresun and Trabzon.

Reduction: 10% on return tickets. No charge for children up to 4 and 50% reduction for children from 4-12, students and journalists. (There are no reduction on meal prices.)

BY RAIL

The wide network of the Turkish State Railways connects most major cities. The trains have couchettes, sleeping cars, and restaurant cars offering first and second class service. Prices vary according to wagon type and distance, between US$3.50 and US$22.50.

Reductions of 20% for return tickets; 10% for students; 30% for groups of more than 15 persons.

BY ROAD

The 41,000 km of asphalt highways are well maintained and easy to drive on. The roads denoted as 'stabilised' are of gravel chippings laid ready for asphalt. Coming from Europe, the crossing of the Bosphorus to Asia has been greatly speeded up by the completion of the Istanbul by-pass and the Bogazici Bridge, leading to the Istanbul-Izmir express road (now completed up to Gabze). The three great axis roads traversing

Turkey are those to Syria and the Lebanon (E-5), Iraq (E-24) and Iran (E-23).

Turkish road signs conform to the International Protocol on Road Signs. Archaeological and historical sites are indicated by yellow signposts.

ACCOMMODATION

A certain number of the hotels throughout the country are registered with the Ministry of Culture and Tourism, which means that they abide by certain regulations and standards of facilities, and these are given the name 'touristic'. There are other establishments registered with local authorities and these too correspond to a certain standard as regards facilities and services.

The government rates hotels under the headings–Luxury (HL), First Class (H1), through to Fourth Class (H4). For example the Hilton and Sheraton are HL, and an H4 would probably be quite small, but with private showers and central heating.

At the seaside resorts and tourist centres of the Mediterranean and Aegean coasts, there a number of motels which generally offer satisfactory facilities (restaurants, private beach, and all mooring facilities) and also some holiday villages of large capacity and high standing.

Prices vary according to standard of accommodation, season in which you travel, and the size of the city in which you are staying. There are many package holidays available from the U.K. An example is air travel and two week's accommodation in an H4 hotel in Fethiye, with bed and breakfast for £309 in high season and £245 in low season.

Camping

The camping grounds registered with the Ministry of Culture and Tourism are still few in number, but they are all situated on the principal routes, near towns and tourist centres. The camping sites of the Mocamp Kervansaray chain, modern equivalents of the old caravanserais, are very comfortable and often have restaurants and occasionally chalets with rooms, and some have private beaches.

These camping sites are generally open from April or May until October. Camping outside of official sites is always possible, but not recommended.

Restaurants

There is a large choice of restaurants in Turkey. There are international class restaurants in the main cities, and everywhere in the country a large number of small popular restaurants offer simple but tasty dishes for moderate prices (£4 per person for dinner, including wine). At most of the establishments along the road there are lambs roasted on a revolving spit, salads and fresh vegetables with rice. If you cannot understand the names of the dishes, you can always go the kitchen and choose from the pots.

SHOPPING

Shopping is one of the advantages of a trip to Turkey and the variety of Turkish crafts means that you end up buying something. Alongside the modern objects, traditional handicrafts from villages and provinces can be found. The most popular objects for the tourist are the carpets, but the varied leather and suede goods, copper and bronze wares, silver, ceramics, handicrafts and embroidery, as well as Turkish meerschaum and onyx are on many people's lists. Backgammon is, generally speaking, the national Turkish game and boards made from inlaid wood with silver or mother-of-pearl are very popular with tourists.

It is best to look around and take note of various prices before you decide to buy, and do not make a counter-offer unless you intend to purchase. It is considered bad manners to barter and agree on a price and then not buy. Sometimes a shopkeeper will say a price is his best, and you will only know it is if you have checked the prices at other shops. In some shops you will be offered coffee, tea or a soft drink as you talk about the goods and prices. This should be accepted and does not mean that you have to purchase their goods.

POPULAR CUSTOMS
Hospitality

Hospitality (Turk Misafirperverligi) is one of the corner-stones of the Turkish way of life. Following Koranic tenets and his naturally friendly instincts, the Turk is a most gracious and generous host. Even the poorest peasant feels bound to honour his guest 'misafir' in the best possible manner. Hospitality is taken to such lengths that a foreigner often feels he is suffering from a surfeit of it, after being plied with food and drinks for hours and being unable to refuse anything lest he hurt his host's feelings. The Turk also makes every effort to converse no matter what the linguistic barriers might be. While most middle class Turks speak at least one European language, even the uneducated bravely struggle to make themselves understood and with remarkable success.

Turkish Coffee Houses

Even the smallest Turkish village has its coffee house or 'kahve' where men can talk, sip coffee and play the national game of backgammon 'tavia'. In Istanbul especially, men can still be seen smoking their hubble bubble pipes 'nargile' in these coffee houses.

Turkish Baths

Owing to the emphasis placed on cleanliness by Islam, there have been public bath houses 'hamam' in Turkey since medieval times. There are separate baths for men and women, or when there is only one bath house in the town, different days are allocated to men and women. After entering the 'hamam' and leaving your clothes in a cubicle, you proceed, wrapped in a towel 'pestemal' to the 'gobek tasi' a large heated stone where you perspire and are rubbed down by a bath attendant. If the heat proves too much, you can retire to a cooler room for a while. This method of bathing is most refreshing and many of the old marble baths are very interesting architecturally. Some of the most interesting Turkish baths for tourists are:

Cagaloglu Hamami, Hilaliahmer Cad. (near the Blue Mosque), Istanbul.

Galatasaray Hamami, Istiklal Cad. Suterazi Sok. 24, Istanbul.

TIPPING

It is expected that tips will be given in restaurants, even if a service charge has been added to the bill. 5% of the bill should be left for the person who served you. If there is no service charge 10% is considered adequate.

Generally speaking anyone who performs a service expects a tip, with the exception of taxi divers.

ISTANBUL

Istanbul, the only city in the world to be built on two continents, stands on the shores of the Istanbul Bogazi where the waters of the Black Sea mingle with the Sea of Marmara and the famous Golden Horn. Here on this splendid site Istanbul guards the precious relics of the three empires of which she has been the capital; a unique link between East and West, between past and present.

Istanbul is an historic city, fascinating and vividly alive. Beneath the unchanging skyline of her domes and minarets there is the continual bustle and movement of the crowd, the rumbling of vehicles along the ancient cobbled streets, the incessant coming and going of the ferries and the cries of street sellers mingling with the sounds of shipping in the busy port.

In Istanbul every year in June and July, the International Istanbul Arts Festival is held.

HOW TO GET THERE

By Air–There are flights from almost every capital and major city in the world to Istanbul's Ataturk Airport.

By Rail–From Europe there are train connections to Sirkeci Station, and from the Middle East and Asia to Haydarpasa Station.

By Road–The E-5 Highway from Europe comes to Turkey, generally via the Kapikule frontier between Turkey and Bulgaria. The E-5 (South) comes via the Ipsala border crossing. Parking stations–Kat Otoparki, Karakoy (opposite the maritime quay), Opera Garaji, Taksim Square (near the Cultural Centre), Sheraton Hotel, Taksim Square, Cukurova Garaji (opposite the Sisli mosque), Aksaray Akin Garaji, Harikazadeler Sok. 2, Laleli.

By Sea–Istanbul is also a port for cruise lines from all parts of the world.

ACCOMMODATION

There is a large number of hotels in Istanbul ranging from Luxury to Fourth Class. A few names and addresses:

Divan (HL), Cumhuriyet Cad. 2 Sisli, Tel. 146 40 21; Etap Marmara (HL), Taksim Meydani Taksim, Tel. 144 88 50; Hilton (HL), Cumhuriyet Cad. Harbiye, Tel. 146 70 50; Sheraton (HL),

Taksim Parki Taksim, Tel. 148 90 00.
Etap Istanbul (H1), Mesrutiyet Cad. Tepebasi, Tel. 144 80 80;
Istanbul Dedeman (H1), Yildiz Posta Cad. 50, Esentepe, Tel. 172
88 00; Perapalas (H1), Mesrutiyet Cad. 98/100, Tepebasi, Tel. 145
22 30 (US$85 ppn);
Akgun (H2), Ordu Cad. Haznedar Sok. 6, Tel. 528 02 61-10;
Dilson (H2), Siraselviler Cad. 49, Taksim, Tel. 143 20 32; Keban
(H2), Siraselviler 51, Taksim, Tel. 143 33 10.
Barin (H3), Fevziye Cad. 25, Sehzadebasi, Tel. 522 84 26; Doru
(H3), Gencturk Cad. 44, Laleli, Tel. 526 59 05; Harem (H3),
Ambar Sok. 1, Selimiye-Uskudar, Tel. 333 20 25.
Agan (H4), Safettin Pasa Sok. 6, Sirkeci, Tel. 527 85 50; Florida
(H4), Fevziye Cad, 38, Laleli, Tel. 528 10 21/22; Italya (H4),
Seferbostan Sok. 2/4, Tel. 144 80 73.

Student Accommodation
Hotels-Akdeniz, 7 Hoci Tahsinbey Sokak, Tel. (05)276 190,
(US$3 double); Engin, Rihtim Tayyareci Sami Sok, 17, Kadikoy,
Tel. 336 47 27 (US$10 double); Hakan, Gencturk Cad. 9, Laleli,
Aksaray, Tel. 527 48 88 (US$10 double); Petek Pansiyon,
Fenerbahce Alptekin Sok. 4, Kadikoy, Tel. 336 22 59 (US$8
double).
Topkapi Ataturk Student Centre, Londra Asfalti, Cevizlibag
Duragi, Topkapi, Istanbul, Tel. 527 02 80
Kadirga Student Hostel, Comertier Sokak, No. 6,
Kumpkapi-Istanbul, Tel. 528 24 80/1
Ortakoy Student Hostel for Girls, Palanga Cad, No. 20, Ortakoy,
Istanbul, Tel. 161 73 76

Camping
Atakoy Mokamp Sahil Yolu, Tel 572 49 61
Yesilyurt Kamping, Sahil Yolu 2, Yesilkoy, Tel. 573 84 08
Kervansaray Kartaltepe Mokamp, Cobancesme Mevkii, Tel. 575
19 91

TOURIST INFORMATION OFFICES

Karakoy Maritime Station, Tel. 149 57 76
Entrance to Hilton Hotel, Tel. 133 05 92-93
Ataturk Airport, Tel. 573 73 99/31 73
Sultanahmet Divanyolu Cad. Sultanahmet, Tel. 522 49 03
Yalova, Iskele Meydani, Tel 21 08

LOCAL TRANSPORT

The cheapest, but slow, means of transport is the bus. On the

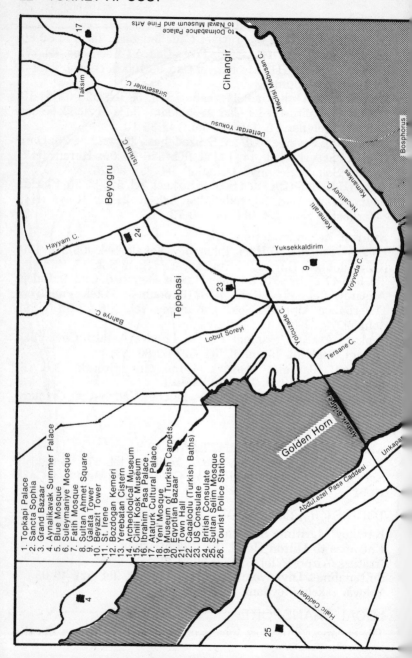

1. Topkapi Palace
2. Sancta Sophia
3. Grand Bazaar
4. Aynalikavak Summer Palace
5. Blue Mosque
6. Suleymaniye Mosque
7. Fatih Mosque
8. Sultan Ahmet Square
9. Galata Tower
10. Beyazit Tower
11. St. Irene
12. Bozdogan Kemeri
13. Yerebatan Cistern
14. Archeological Museum
15. Cinili Kosk Museum
16. Ibrahim Pasa Palace
17. Ataturk Cultural Palace
18. Yeni Mosque
19. Museum of Turkish Carpets
20. Egyptian Bazaar
21. Town Hall
22. Cagaloglu (Turkish Baths)
23. US Consulate
24. British Consulate
25. Sultan Selim Mosque
26. Tourist Police Station

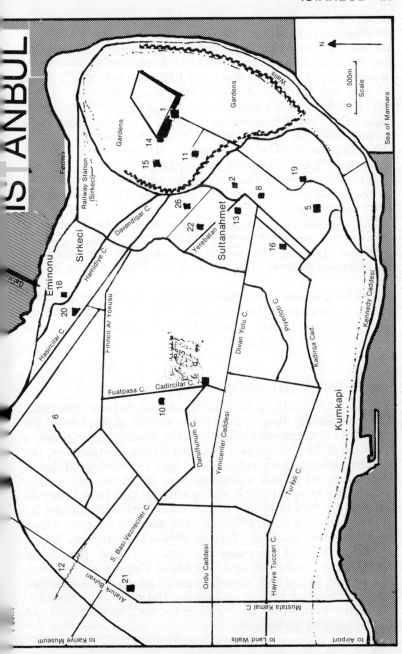

ISTANBUL

N

Scale
0   500m

Sea of Marmara

Walls

Gardens

Gardens

Gardens

1

14

15

11

2

19

8

26

22

5

13

Yerebatan

16

Sultanahmet

Railway Station
(Sirkeci)

Davendigar C.

Hamidiye C.

Fuatpasa C.

Cadircilar C.

Sirkeci

Eminonu

18

20

Hasircilar C.

Firincil Ar Yokusu

10

Kumkapi

6

Divan Yolu C.

Piyenoti C.

Kadirga Cad.

Kennedy Caddesi

Darulfunum C.

Yeniceriler Caddesi

Turlali C.

S. Basi-Vezneciler C.

12

21

Ordu Caddesi

Ataturk Bulvari

Hayriye Tuccari C.

Mustafa Kemal C.

to Kariye Museum

to Land Walls

to Airport

European side the main bus lines start from Taksim square, Eminonu (near the Galata Bridge) and Beyazit (near the covered Bazaar). On the Asian side, there are departures from Uskudar and Kadikoy. Bus tickets are sold at designated kiosks. There is also a regular bus service every half hour between Ataturk Airport and the THY Airline Terminal at Sishane.

The 'dolmus' is a practical and cheap means of transport, especially when compared to the taxi. Each passenger pays according to the distance travelled and the fares are fixed by the municipality. The main dolmus stations are at Taksim, Eminonu, Sirkeci, Uskudar and Kadikoy.

Taxi ranks are everywhere in the city and are easily recognised by their chequered black and yellow bands. They are equipped with taxi meters.

The steamer is a practical, enjoyable and cheap means of transport. There are several departures from Eminonu to the Istanbul Bogazi, the Golden Horn, Uskudar, Kadikoy, Haydarpasa (railway station) and the Princes Islands and Yalova.

The local trains that depart from Sirkeci Station go to the camping grounds on the European side of the Sea of Marmara and those that depart from Haydarpasa Station serve the suburbs on the Asian side.

ENTERTAINMENT AND DINING

Istanbul is well catered for in terms of food and entertainment. The traditionally Turkish form is the 'gazino' night clubs which provide entertainment throughout the dinner, ranging from a selection of Turkish songs to the belly-dance. Alongside are the modern discotheques, cabaret and jazz clubs of the Taksim-Harbiye district. The traditional fare, in almost any dining establishment is the 'meze', the special Turkish hors d'oeuvres followed by freshly grilled fish or meat, and accompanied by Turkish wines or the traditional 'raki' anisette which is drunk with water and ice. Some Turkish dishes: the tempting 'midye dolmasi' (stuffed mussels) 'Tarama' (smoked fishroe in mayonnaise), 'cerkez tavugu' (Circassian chicken–cold chicken in a walnut sauce) and 'yaprak dolmasi' (stuffed grape leaves). Generally the fish is fresh, and among the most tasty are 'lufer' (blue fish), 'kilic' (sword fish), 'kalkan' (turbot), 'levrek' (bass) and 'barbunya' (red mullet).

POINTS OF INTEREST
PALACES

TOPKAPI PALACE. Overlooking the Istanbul Bogazi and the Golden Horn stands the maze of buildings that was the great palace of the Ottoman sultans from the 15th to the 19th century. The first courtyard is a magnificent wooded garden. On the right of the second court, shaded by cypress and plane trees is the palace kitchen, now housing an exquisite collection of Chinese porcelain. The Harem, beautifully restored, was the secluded quarters of the wives and concubines of the Sultan. In the third court is the Hall of Audience of the Sultan, the library of Sultan Ahmet III, an exhibition of robes worn by the sultans and their families, the famous jewels of the Imperial Treasury and lastly an exhibition of miniatures. In the fourth court is the Pavilion of the Holy Mantle enshrining relics of the Prophet Mohammed. Open every day except Tuesday.

DOLMABAHCE PALACE. Built in the mid-19th century by Sultan Abdulmecit, it has a six hundred metre frontage onto the Istanbul Bogazi. The most important part of the palace is the vast reception salon supported by 56 columns with a huge crystal chandelier of 750 lamps weighing 4.5 tonnes. The Bird Pavilion houses birds from all over the world and is unique to this palace. Ataturk, founder of the Turkish Republic, who died here on November 10, 1938, used this as his residence. Open every day except Monday and Thursday.

BEYLERBEYI PALACE. On the Asian side of the Istanbul Botazi built by Sultan Abdulaziz in 1865 of white marble, it possesses a beautiful garden with magnolia trees. It was used as a summer residence of the Sultans and a guest house for visiting foreign dignitaries. Open every day except Monday and Thursday.

GOKSU PALACE (Kucuksu). It takes its name from the famous streams nearby; built by Adbulmecit between 1856-57 and used as a summer residence. Open every day except Monday and Thursday.

YILDIZ PALACE. A complex of pavilions, a palace and a mosque built over a long period of time and by several sultans but completed by Abdulhamit 11 at the end of the 19th century. It is set in a very large garden of flowers, plants and trees brought from many parts of the world. Situated on the top of a hill, it has one of the most beautiful panoramic views of Istanbul and the water.

AYNALI KAVAK SUMMER PALACE. Originally built in the 17th century and restored by many sultans after that, it takes it present name (Mirrored Poplar) from the time of the installation of the mirrors (1718) given as a gift by the Venediks. This palace on the Golden Horn is one of the most beautiful examples of traditional architecture.

IHLAMUR PAVILION. Built between 1839-61 takes its name from the linden trees that grow in abundance in the garden. The Merasim Pavilion was the scene of official ceremonies and the Maiyet Pavilion housed the sultan's entourage, and on occasions, his harem.

MOSQUES

SULTAN AHMET MOSQUE (1609-1616). Facing Sancta Sophia is the imperial mosque of Sultan Ahmet 1. Built by the architect Mehmet, it is known as the Blue Mosque because of its interior decoration of blue Iznik tiles.

SULEYMANIYE MOSQUE. The Mosque of Suleyman the Magnificent is considered the most splendid of all imperial mosques in Istanbul. It was built between 1550 and 1557 by the architect Sinan whose dearest wish was to surpass the builders of Sancta Sophia. Standing on a hill it is conspicuous by its great size, emphasised by the four minarets rising one from each corner of the courtyard. Inside, the mihrab (prayer-niche) and the mimber (pulpit) are of finely carved marble, and there are fine stained glass windows. Adjoining the mosque are theological schools, a school of medicine, a soup kitchen and hospice for the poor, a caravanserai and a turkish bash.

RUSTEM PASA MOSQUE. Built in 1561 the mosque of Rustem Pasa beside the Golden Horn was designed by the architect Sinan on the orders of Rustem Pasa, Grand Visier and son-in-law of Suleyman.

FATIH MOSQUE. This imperial mosque constructed between 1463 and 1470 bears the name of the conqueror of Istanbul. Standing on top of one of the hills of Istanbul, it is notable for its vast size and the great complex of religious foundations surrounding it.

EYUP MOSQUE. The Great Mosque of Eyup is situated

outside the walls near the Golden Horn, where Eyup, standard-bearer of the Prophet Mohammed, died in an assault on Constantinople in 670. His tomb is greatly venerated and attracts many pilgrims. It was the first mosque built after the conquest of Istanbul.

YENI MOSQUE. Built between 1597 and 1663, the Yeni Cami or New Mosque, located at the Eminonu side of the Galata Bridge is one ofthe best known sights of Istanbul. An elegant fountain for ablutions stands in the large courtyard, and the sultan's section is decorated with marvellous Iznik tiles.

MONUMENTS

SULTAN AHMET SQUARE. In front of the Blue Mosque is the site of the ancient Hippodrome, the scene of chariot races and the centre of Byzantine civic life. Of the monuments which once decorated it only three remain, the Obelisk of Teodosius, the bronze Serpentine Column and the Obelisk of Bricks.

AHMET III FOUNTAIN. Standing at the entrance to Topkapi Palace, and built in 1729 as a gift to Ahmet III, it is one of the most magnificent free-standing fountains. Highly ornamented, covered with a pointed roof with deep eaves, it is a fine example of fountain architecture.

RUMELI HISARI. The Rumelian Fortress built by Fatih Sultan Mehmet in 1452 prior to the conquest of Istanbul, was completed in only four months. One of the most striking works of military architecture anywhere in the world, it is now used as the setting for some of the shows of the Istanbul Festival. Open every day except Monday.

GALATA TOWER. This huge tower was built by the Genoese in 1348, and is 62 metres high. There is a wonderful view of the Golden Horn and the Istanbul Bogazi. It now houses a restaurant, night club and a bar.

BEYAZIT TOWER. Situated in the grounds of the Istanbul University, this tower is 85 metres and was built by Mahmut 11 in 1828 as a fire tower.

THE ISTANBUL LAND WALLS. Built in the 5th century by the Emperor Theodosius II, these walls stretch 7 km from the Sea of Marmara to the Golden Horn. With their many towers and bastions, they were once the mightiest fortifications in Christendom.

BOZDOGAN KEMERI (Aqueduct of Valens). Built by the Emperor Valens in 368 AD, this aqueduct supplied the Byzantine and later the Ottoman palaces with water. About 900 metres of the double tier arches remain.

KIZKULESI. Known also as Leanders Tower, it is situated on a tiny islet at the entrance to Istanbul harbour. Although first constructed in the 12th century, the present building dates from the 18th century.

MUSEUMS

AYASOFYA MUSEUM (Sancta Sophia). This ancient basilica built by Constantine the Great and reconstructed by Justinian in the 6th century, is one of the greatest marvels of architecture of all time. Its immense dome rises 55 metres above the ground and is 31 metres in diameter. The beautiful decorations include the Byzantine mosaics. Open every day except Monday.

KARIYE MUSEUM. The 11th century St. Saviour in Chlora is, after Sancta Sophia, the most important Byzantine monument in Istanbul. The walls are decorated with superb 14th century frescoes and mosaics on a gold background. The church is a remarkable museum of Byzantine art. Here you will find a quiet carefully-tended garden where you can sip your tea or coffee. Open every day except Tuesday.

ST. IRENE MUSEUM. St. Irene was the first church built by the Byzantines in the city; rebuilt by Constantine in the 4th century, the site is reputedly that of a pre-Christian temple. Preparations are being made for it to be a mosaic museum. Open every day except Wednesday.

YEREBATAN CISTERN. To the west of St. Sophia is the Byzantine cistern (6th century) known as the Yerebatan Saray or Underground Palace. Fine brick vaulting is supported by 336 Corinthian columns. Open every day except Tuesday.

THE ARCHEOLOGICAL MUSEUMS. These are situated at the boundary of the first court of Topkapi Palace. The very rich collection of antiques in the Archeological Museum includes the celebrated Sarcophagus of Alexander. The Museum of the Ancient Orient displays antiques from the Hatti, Hittite, Assyrian, Babylonian and Summerian civilisations. Open every day except Monday.

CINILI KOSK (The Museum of Turkish Ceramics). The Kosk

or Pavilion was built by Fatih Sultan Mehmet in the 15th century. It contains beautiful Iznik tiles from the 16th century and fine examples of Seljuk and Ottoman tiles. Open every day except Monday.

IBRAHIM PASA PALACE (The Museum of Turkish and Islamic Art). Built in 1524 by Ibrahim Pasa, Grand Vizier of Suleyman the Magnificent, it is the grandest private residence ever built in the Ottoman Empire. It is now used as a museum, containing many beautiful Turkish and Persian miniatures, Seljuk tiles, korans and antique carpets. Open every day except Monday.

NAVAL MUSEUM. In the Besiktas neighbourhood, it contains the great imperial caiques that were used to row the sultan across the Istanbul Bogazi, and many interesting exhibits from Ottoman naval history. Open Wednesday to Sunday.

MILITARY MUSEUM. The exhibits from Ottoman military history include the great field tents used on campaigns, and shows by 'mehter takim' the Ottoman military bands. Open Wednesday to Sunday.

ATATURK MUSEUM. The house where Ataturk lived in Sisli, containing personal effects of Ataturk. Open Monday to Friday.

SADBERK HANIM MUSEUM. Dedicated to old Turkish arts and handicrafts, situated on the Istanbul Bogazi at Buyukdere. Open every day except Wednesday.

MUSEUM OF FINE ARTS. At Besiktas, one of the best museums in Turkey with paintings and sculptures from the end of the 19th century to the modern period. Open Wednesday to Sunday.

THE MUSEUM OF TURKISH CARPETS. Near the Sultan Ahmet Mosque, it contains a fine collection of Turkish carpets and kilims including some of the oldest examples. Open Tuesday to Saturday.

ISTANBUL BOGAZI (BOSPHORUS)

A stay in Istanbul should not be completed without the traditional and unforgettable excursion by boat along the Istanbul Bogazi, the winding straits separating Europe and Asia. Along its shores is a surprising mixture of the past and present, modern hotels and 'yali', ancient villas of wood, admist

palaces of marble, fortresses and small holiday fishing villages.
The best way of seeing the Istanbul Bogazi is to board one of
the passenger boats that regularly zigzag up along the shores,
starting from Eminonu and stopping alternately on the Asian
and European side. The round trip excursion takes about seven
hours and the fare is reasonable.

During the excursion you will see the Palace of Dolmabahce.
Further along are the parks and imperial pavilions of the Yildiz
Palace. Here in the park grounds are the Malta and Cadir
Pavilions, now cafes. Spanning the water and linking Europe
and Asia for the first time is a bridge, one of the longest in the
world. Immediately after the bridge, on the Asian side is
Beylerbeyi, a marble palace. From the water, Camlica Hill, the
highest point of Istanbul can be seen. Here one gets a good view
of Istanbul. Just across on the European side are the contrasting
elements of old and new such as the Ottoman wooden villas or
'yali' of Arnavutkoy and the luxury apartments of Bebek. Facing
each other across the straits are the fortresses of Rumeli Hisari
and Anadolu Hisari. Just before the Anadolu Hisari is the
Goksu Palace, sometimes known as the Kucuksu Palace. On the
European side is the Emirgan Park with its pavilions famous
for tulips, and the annual tulip festival. In this park are three
cafe pavilions; Sari, Pembe and Beyaz. The Beyaz Pavilion is
also used as a concert hall. Opposite, on the Asian shore is
Kanlica, with its elegant villas. At Cubkuklu, shortly after
Kanlica is the Hidiv Palace set in wooded gardens where
concerts and conferences are now held. On the the European side
yachts can be moored at the bay of Tarabya.

You can contact agencies through your hotel which specialise
in the organising 'mini-cruises' or trips by car along the shore.

SURROUNDING ATTRACTIONS

THE PRINCES ISLANDS. These nine islands are famous for
their beautiful pinewooded scenery and beaches. The largest is
Buyuk Ada, one hour's journey by ferry departing from
Eminonu. The other popular islands are Kinali, Sedef, Burgaz
and Heybeliada.

FLORYA-ATALPU-FENERBAHCE-SUADIYE-DRAGOS. On
both the European and Asian sides there are summer resorts
with hotels, motels, restaurants, etc. where the Istanbulians
spend their vacation time.

KILYOS. On the European side of the Black Sea, famous for

its long, broad sandy beaches.

BELGRAD ORMANI (Belgrade Forest). The largest forest in and around Istanbul set amongst the Istranca Mountains, a popular picnic spot with the locals. There are seven ancient reservoirs, an aqueduct from Ottoman times as well as natural springs.

POLONEZKOY. On the Asian side, 25km from Beykoz, Polonezkoy was founded in 1873 by a Polish prince who brought refugee and exiled Poles to settle here. The newcomers worked in dairy and poultry, and provided guest-houses. Another favourite week-end picnic place for the locals.

RIVA. A fishing village on the Black Sea coast 30km from Beykoz. Restaurants and simple guest houses are available.

SILE. On the Black Sea, 70km from Uskudar, Sile is famous for its sandy beaches, hotels and fish restaurants.

YALOVA. On the southern shore of Marmara, Yalova is a popular thermal resort known since Roman times for its cures for rheumatism. The main resort is a few kilometres from the town of Yalova. In Yalova itself there are many inexpensive hotels and guest houses. To reach Yalova: ferryboat from Kabatas or Sirkeci-2½ hours; car ferry from Kartal on the Asian side-1½ hours.

SHOPPING

Shopping in Istanbul is one of the main delights of a visit to this city. For something different wander through the colourful bazaars.

For tourists the great 'Kapali Carsi' or Covered Bazaar in the old city is a favourite place. Here in this labyrinth of shops each trade has its own place; the goldsmiths' street, the carpet sellers' street and so on. The best souvenirs are the genuine products of ancient Turkish crafts, such as the hand painted ceramic plates, and the hand-beaten copper and brass ware, trays, water ewers, cauldrons, etc. which make beautiful decorative pieces. There are also the 'heybe' embroidered bags, and the 'yastik' cushions, or the vases, bowls and other objects in fine green or gold onyx, or pipes carved out of soft white meerschaum stone. Leather and suede goods are relatively inexpensive as well.

It is worth looking at the great range of antiques in the Old Bedestan in the Bazaar centre. There is an endless array of antiques and souvenirs: copperware, lamps, jewellery, tiles, silver and glassware.

Behind the Yeni Cami (New Mosque) is another attractive bazaar of a different sort, the Misir Carsisi or Spice Bazaar. Here the air is filled with the enticing aromas of cinnamon, caraway, saffron, mint, thyme and every conceivable spice.

Contrasting with the noisy bustle of the bazaars are the sophisticated shops of the Taksim-Nisantasi-Sisli districts. At Istiklai Caddesi and Cumhuriyet Caddesi, near Taksim, and Rumeli Caddesi in Nisantasi are the most fashionable shops where the most exquisite clothing and jewellery can be found, as well as fine quality leather goods such as suede coats and jackets, and well designed handbags and shoes. On the Asian side of Istanbul at Bahariye Caddesi and on Bagdat Caddesi are similarly modern shopping centres.

In the Kuledibi, Carsikapi, Uskudar and Topkapi districts of Istanbul are busy fleamarkets where one can find an astonishing assortment of goods, both old and new.

BURSA

Bursa stands at the foot of the 2543m Uludag mountain, the mythological Mt. Olympus of Mysia.

Taking its name from Prusias 1, King of Bythinia, Bursa was the capital of the Ottoman Empire (14th century) and has the first examples of the Ottoman culture. Today, surrounded by lush gardens, it is an industrial and commercial centre. On the one hand silk-weaving, towel-making and fruit-growing have much advanced, and on the other its hot springs have become famous.

The special chestnut candy and Iskender kebab are best eaten here.

HOW TO GET THERE
By plane from Istanbul. By bus from all major cities. By ferry boat from Istanbul to Yalova.

ACCOMMODATION
Hotels
Akdogan (H2), Murat Cad. 5, Tel. 247 55-57 (US$30ppn); Celik Palas (H2), Cekirge Cad. 79, Tel. 619 00-0; Anatolia (H2), Zubeyde Hanim Cad., Tel. 671 10; Dilmen (H2), Hamamtar Cad., Tel. 217 01-173; Adapalas (H3), Murat Cad. 21, Tel. 192 00-1; Buyuk Yildiz (H3), Uludag Yolu, Tel. 299 44-45; Diyar (H3), Cekirge Cad 47, Tel. 192 04-5; Gonluferah (H3), Murat Cad. 24, Tel. 179 00-1; Yat (H3), Hamamlar Cad. 31, Tel. 117 20-186 95; Artic (H4), Fevzi Cakmak Cad. 123, Tel. 195 00-1; Dikman (H4), Maksem Cad. 78, Tel. 184 23-20 319; Ilman (H4), Kulturpark Fuar Karsisi 45, Tel. 152 48; Kent (H4), Ataturk Cad. 119, Tel. 187 00-1.

Student-Hasanaga Youth and Boy Scout Hostel, Kucuk Kumla/Gemlik, Tel 289 Kumla/Bursa.

Camping
Kervansaray Kumluk Mokamp, Yalova-bursa Yolu 6km, Tel. 139 95

TOURIST INFORMATION OFFICES
Bursa-Ahmet Hamdi Tanpinar Cad. Saydam Is Merkezi 21, 5. Kat, Tel. 28005.
  Ataturk Cad. 64, Tel. 12359
  Cemal Nadir Cad., Tophane, Tel. 13368.
  Iznik, Kilicaslan Cad. 168, Tel. 1933.

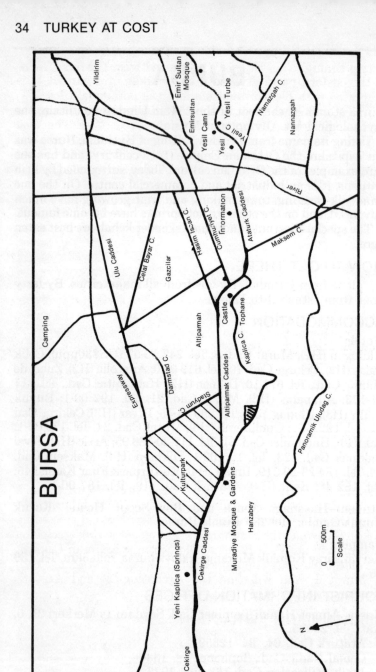

BURSA

Yildirim

Emir Sultan Mosque

Emirsultan

Yesil Cami

Yesil Cami

Yesil Türbe

Namazgah C.

Nannazqah

River

Information

Cumhuriyet C.

Hasim Iscan C.

Gazcilar

Celal Bayar C.

Ulu Caddesi

Ataturk Caddesi

Maksem C.

Camping

Altiparmah

Castle

Kaplica C. Tophane

Darmstad C.

Expressway

Altiparmak Caddesi

Stadyum C.

Panoramik Uludag C.

Kulturpark

Muradiye Mosque & Gardens

Hanzabey

Cekirge Caddesi

Yeni Kaplica (Springs)

Cekirge

0   500m

Scale

N

CITY EXCURSIONS

A trip through this city may be started from the Yesil Turbe in the eastern part; situated in the middle of a garden, it is decorated with blue turquoise and green octagonal tiles.

Yesil Cami, the most famous religious site in Bursa, is decorated from top to bottom with blue-green tiles. The Yesil Medresse has now been turned into a Turkish Art Museum and the whole area is called the Yesil Complex. A visit to the tea garden is something you do not want to overlook.

Further to the east is the Emir Sultan Mosque and walking through a quarter of quaint hold houses you come to Yildirim Beyazit Mosque, one of the first in the Ottoman style. From here, turning to Cumhuriyet Square, the city centre, following Ataturk Caddesi, is the covered bazaar area with its typical little streets, caravanserais and bedestans. Further on is the dome shaped Ulu Mosque in the Ottoman style. This 20-domed mosque is the largest in Bursa. Inside, the fountain, the carved walnut and the rich calligraphic decorations on the walls are eye-catching.

Following Ataturk Caddesi you come to the walls of the castle, the city's most beautiful sight dominating a square where the mausoleums of the founder of the Ottoman Empire Sultan Osman, and Bursa's conqueror Orhan, rise up. At the base of this site be sure to have a cup of tea nestled in an Ottoman setting at the Tophane Cafe, or go up to the Yildiz Tea Garden for the most photographed view of the city. The famous blue-tiled Muradiye Mosque and Muradiye Complex has a garden of cypress trees, roses and magnolias containing the tombs of Murad 11 and his family. Cem Sultan and Sehzade Mustafa are also buried here. Peace and quiet rule in this garden, and at the exit you will find an 18th century Ottoman House Museum.

Further, extending as far as Cekirge are modern thermal springs and hotels alongside old hamams (Turkish baths). Of these the best known is Yeni Kaplica (New Spring) erected by Sultan Suleyman the Magnificent. The oldest spring erected by Justinian is the Eski Kaplica (Old Spring). Again in Cekirge, the oldest religious buildings are the Mosque and Mausoleum of Murat 1. You will find the Archeological and Ataturk Museums worthy of a visit.

SURROUNDING ATTRACTIONS
ULUDAG

This winter sports centre is 36km from Bursa by road, and can also be reached by cable car. This is the largest of the winter sport facilities in Turkey, and has a variety of entertainments which combine to make a marvellous holiday. December to May is best for skiing, and hotels are found at the foot of the ski slopes. Uludag, a national park, is a lovely place to visit in the summer too.

MUDANYA

This is a sea side resort town, 25km from Bursa. The fine fish restaurants and the night clubs are a favourite attraction for the people of Bursa. To see a typical Turkish town for its architecture and street layout you will enjoy Zeytinbagi (Tirilye) 12km from Mundanya.

GEMLIK

Gemlik is on a bay of wide sandy beaches 29km from Bursa. The fish restaurants and accommodation make it a pleasant place to stay.

YALOVA

Yalova on the Bursa-Yalova road passing through Gemlik Bay, is 70km north of Bursa. It has been a city of sulphureous hot water springs for centuries. Cinarcik, 17km away, is a pretty resort town.

IZNIK

Iznik, formerly known as Nicaea, stands 85km to the north-east of Bursa at the eastern tip of Iznik Lake. Along the shore are fish restaurants, hotels and camping sites. Iznik has a long history and was one of the most famous towns of Rome and Byzantium; in 1078 it passed into the hands of the Seljuks and in 1331 into the Ottoman's. From these changes the town has become rich in Islamic monuments. In the 16th century Iznik was famous for the manufacture of tiles. The major mosques and palaces of Turkey are decorated with Iznik tiles.

The walls around the city, the castle towers, and the remains of the Roman gates prove that Iznik was once a major city. In 325 AD the Ecumenical Council was held here in Ayasofya Cathedral, and its structure has stood from that day to this. The famous turquoise tiled Yesil Mosque and the Nilufer Hatun Imareti (now a museum) are among the Islamic monuments to be seen.

CANAKKALE AND DARDANELLES

Canakkale get its name from the 15th century castle built by Fatih Sultan Mehmet, at the narrowest point of the Dardenelles, the straits joining the Sea of Marmara to the Aegean Sea. The castle has been restored, and is still used by the military.

HOW TO GET THERE

The road follows the Marmara coastline via Biga to Canakkale, where it joins the E24. There are bus services from Izmir, Istanbul or Bursa, and boats sail from Istanbul–Gelibolu–Canakkale–Imroz Islands.

TOURIST INFORMATION OFFICE

Iskele Mey 67, Tel. 1187.

ACCOMMODATION

Hotels
Anafartalar (H3), Anafartalar, Tel. 454-55; Truva (H3), Yaliboyu, Tel. 1024-1886; Bakir (H4), Yali Cad. 12, Tel. 4088-89-90.
Motel
Mola, Guzelyali Koyu, Tel. 22.

EXCURSIONS

GELIBOLU (Gallipoli) lies across the straits from Canakkale. It was here during the second world war that the allied forces were defeated by the Turks, who were led by Mustafa Kemal (Ataturk). A monument to his victory is on the shores of the peninsula, and the allied cemeteries are at the tip of the peninsula.

TROY. The ancient ruins of Troy are 27 km southwest of Canakkale. There have actually been nine cities uncovered, the earliest dating back to 3000 BC. There is some controversy as to which level is the city described in the Iliad. Although it may take some imagination to visualise the original cities from the ruins, a trip to this area should not be missed. There is a well sign-posted and arrowed walk through the excavations, as well as tourist guides.

AYVALIK, with its much indented coastline covered with pine forests, and the 23 islands of various sizes scattered around in the gulf, maintains the largest olive tree plantations in Turkey. Ayvalik is situated on the E24 between Canakkale and Izmir. Besides its natural attractions, Ayvalik is important for its cultural and architectural values, and is one of the most attractive tourist centres.

Three miles from the centre of town is the island of Alibey (Cunda) which can be reached either by road or by motorboat that is available at any time of day. A promenade from the centre of town leads towards the picturesque Ayvalik Marina, where tourists coming by yachts are accommodated.

CAMLIK is situated 3 km south of Ayvalik. Turn right off the road leading south and you come to the hill called Seytan Sofrasi (Devil's Dining Table). From the top of this hill there is a panoramic view of the Ayvalik islands. At Sarmisakli, 8 km to the south, there is a 7 km long beach and a number of hotels and camping grounds.

THE GULF OF EDREMIT. Situated on the Edremit gulf, known as the 'Olive Riviera', is the town of Edremit which has been the setting of many mythological legends. On the slopes of the hills are hot springs and thermal baths, and many game animals can be found in the forest which ends at Kaz Dagi (Mt. Ida). Along the coast are the holiday towns of Oren, Akcay, Altinoluk and Kucukkuyu, all joined by roads, and in the summer there are scheduled ferry connections between Oren and Akcay.

IZMIR

Izmir is the 3rd largest city in Turkey, and the NATO headquarters for the south-east sector. It is situated along the shores of a very large bay sheltered by mountains encircling the city. Contributing to the city's renown as 'Beautiful Izmir' are the bay, the mildness of the climate tempered in summer by refreshing sea breezes, the broad avenues lined with palm trees, houses lying in terraces up the hillsides and above all, the liveliness of the city.

HOW TO GET THERE

There is a daily train service from Ankara, and from Bandirma connecting with the boat ferry from Istanbul. THY has some direct flights from Europe, and daily flights from Istanbul and Ankara. The E24 and E23 meet at Izmir.

ACCOMMODATION

Hotels
Buyuk Efes (HL), Gaziosmanpasa Bul. 1, Tel. 14 43 00-29 (US$65 ppn); Etap Izmir (H1), Cumhuriyet Bul. 138, Tel. 14 42 90-99; Kismet (H1), 1377 Sok. 9, Tel. 21 70 50-52; Anba (H2), Cumhuriyet Bul. 124, Tel. 14 43 80-4; Izmir Palas (H2), Vasif Cinar Bul. 2, Tel. 21 55 83; Karaca (H2), 1379 Sok. 55, Tel. 14 44 45; Kilim (H2), Ataturk Bul., Tel. 14 53 40-5; Kaya (H3), Gaziosmanpasa Bul. 45 Cankaya, Tel. 13 97 71-3; Babadan (H4), Gaziosmanpasa Bul. 50, Tel. 13 96 40-3; Billur (H4), Basmane Mey. 783, Tel. 13 62 50.

TOURIST INFORMATION OFFICE

Alsancak, Ataturk Cad. 418, Tel. 22 02 07-08.
G.O.P. Bul. Buyuk Efes Oteli Alti 1/C, Tel. 14 21 47.

POINTS OF INTEREST

Izmir, the ancient Smyrna, is not really a tourist centre, but it is a good base for the interesting Aegean sights. The city was almost completely destroyed by fire in 1922, and has been rebuilt as a modern city.

The Izmir Trade Fair, from August 20 to September 20 each year, is the most important in the Eastern Mediterranean. The

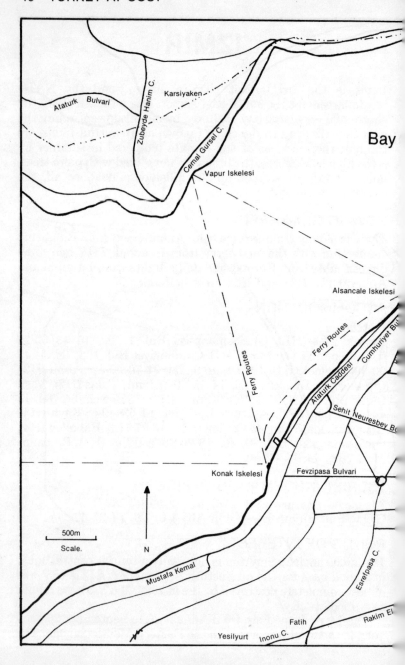

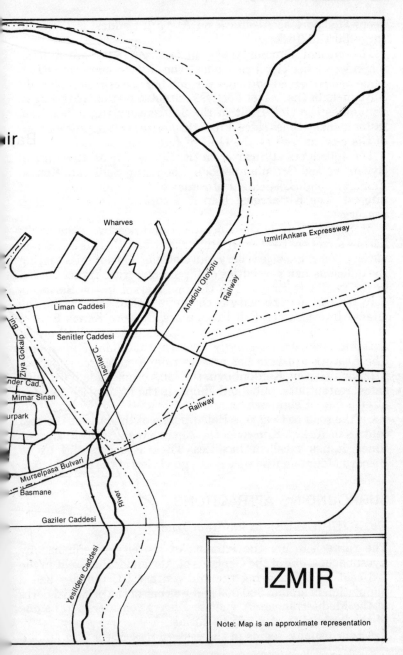

ir

Wharves

Izmir/Ankara Expressway

Liman Caddesi

Senitler Caddesi

Ziya Gokalp Bulv.

Anadolu Otoyolu

Railway

nder Cad.

Iscler C.

Mimar Sinan

urpark

Railway

Murselpasa Bulvari

Basmane

River

Gaziler Caddesi

Yeslidere Caddesi

IZMIR

Note: Map is an approximate representation

deepwater port at Alsanack on Ataturk Caddesi is the main cargo port of Turkey.

The ancient remains that can be seen today are a small reminder of the city's rich past. The Roman agora possesses some well preserved porticoes surrounding the central esplanade.

Kadifekale, the 'Velvet Fortress', situated on top of Mt. Pagos, dominates the city. Built in the 3rd century BC, it has been restored many times since. From this fortress a magnificent view of the city, as well as the Gulf of Izmir, can be seen.

The aqueducts at Sirinyer on the Kemer (Meles) River are of Byzantine and Ottoman periods. The Hisar, Sadirvan, Konak, Kemeralti and Salepcioglu Mosques of Ottoman origin, are of interest. The Kizlaragasi Han is a caravanserai of the 18th century.

At Konak there is the clocktower and nearby is the lively, narrow streets of the Kemeralti Bazaar where there is an infinite variety of antiques, jewellery and clothing. Do not miss tasting the delicious fish specialties of Cipura and fried Tranca served in the quaint restaurants in the fish market in the Bazaar.

In the centre of the city is the huge Kultur Park where the annual International Fair takes place. Close to Konak Square is the Archeological Museum containing a collection of antiquities dating from early western Anatolian civilisations. The Ataturk Museum has articles from a more recent period.

Izmir's elegent Kordonboyu, the long promenade lined with cafes, restaurants, pubs and shops, is the ideal place to relax after a day of sight-seeing.

On the road to Cesme is Balcova, one of the largest thermal centres in Turkey. Known as the Agamemnon Baths in ancient times, it has excellent facilities. There is a cabin-lift up to Balcova Mountain where there is a good view of the Bay of Izmir.

SURROUNDING ATTRACTIONS

EFES (EPHESUS)–73 km from Izmir.

The ruins here are the remains of the city established by Lyssimachos, one of the Generals of Alexander the Great in the 3rd century BC. During the 2nd century BC the city had a population of around 300,000 and was one of the principal ports of the Mediterranean. A visit to Efes is considered to be one of the highlights of a trip to Turkey.

A tour usually begins in the eastern part of the city around

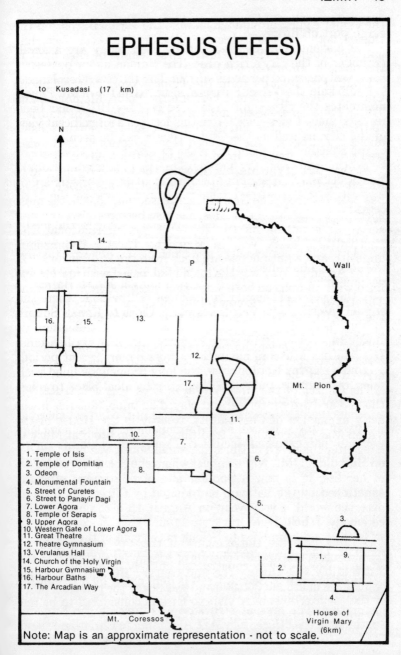

EPHESUS (EFES)

to Kusadasi (17 km)

N

14.

P

Wall

16. 15. 13.

12.

17.

Mt. Pion

11.

10.

7.

8.

6.

5.

3.

1. 9.

2.

4.

1. Temple of Isis
2. Temple of Domitian
3. Odeon
4. Monumental Fountain
5. Street of Curetes
6. Street to Panayir Dagi
7. Lower Agora
8. Temple of Serapis
9. Upper Agora
10. Western Gate of Lower Agora
11. Great Theatre
12. Theatre Gymnasium
13. Verulanus Hall
14. Church of the Holy Virgin
15. Harbour Gymnasium
16. Harbour Baths
17. The Arcadian Way

Mt. Coressos

House of
Virgin Mary
(6km)

Note: Map is an approximate representation - not to scale.

the Upper Agora, around which were the Varius Baths and the Odeion, both from the 2nd century, the Prytaneion or Town Hall, and the Temple of Domitian, the first temple of Efes built in the name of an emperor (81-96 AD)

Leading westwards from the Upper Agora is the famous Curetes Street. Of interest here are the Pollio, Memmius, and Trajan Fountains, the elegant facade of the Temple of Hadrian, the Scholastika Baths and the Hercules Gate. Set on the hillside above the street are the Terraced Houses, restored, containing well preserved frescoes from the 2nd century AD.

At the start of the Marble Street is the Lower Agora, and to its left the Celsus Library with its very elaborate facade, which has been restored. The Grand Theatre, seating 25,000, the most spectacular monument of Efes, has also been restored and now serves as a setting for the shows of the International Efes Festival held every year in May. The Theatre Gymnasium opposite, and a bath house are both from the 2nd century AD.

The Arcadian Way was the main road, paved with marble and lined with columns on both sides, that stretched from the Grand Theatre to the old port, now totally silted up. On this road were the Four Evangelists Monument, four columns on which stood statues of the evangelists.

Down by the ancient harbour is the Harbour Gymnasium and Baths, constructed in order to receive with dignity those who arrived from the sea.

The Church of the Holy Virgin in Efes, was constructed in the 2nd and 3rd centuries, and played an important role in the early expansion of Christianity. Nearby is the House of the Virgin Mary. According to tradition, St. John brought Mary to Efes after the death of Christ. A small house was built for her on Bulbuldagi (Mt. Nightingale) where she spent the last days of her life. It is now a popular site of pilgrimage officially sanctioned by the Vatican, and visited by Christians from all over the world. Every year on August 15 a commemoration ceremony is held here.

On the road from Efes to Selcuk is the ruin of the Temple of Artemis. Once numbered amongst the Seven Wonders of the Ancient World, it was constructed entirely of marble.

The little town of Selcuk itself is dominated by a Byzantine citadel overlooking the Basilica of St. John, presently under restoration. The present structure was built by the Emperor Justinian in the 6th century AD. According to Christian legend, St. John lived on this hilltop and on his death was buried here.

Interior Topkapi Museum, Istabul,

Istanbul, Rumel Hisari(Walls)

Next to the basilica is the Isa Bey Mosque with its typically Seljuk style portal.

The Selcuk Archeological Museum has only recently been enlarged and newly arranged to display the many impressive works of art recovered from and around Efes.

BERGAMA (PERGAMUM)

The ancient city of Pergamum was a great centre of culture, and was the rival of Ephesus in the field of commerce, and of Alexandria and Antioch in that of the letters and the arts.

A tour of the site starts with the Asclepieion located to the south-west of the lower city. This well known sanctuary was dedicated to the god of health, Asclepios. Places to be noted in the same area are the circular temples of Telesphorus and Asclepios, the restored theatre and the library. The annual Bergama Festival is held in the theatre. In the town of Bergama are the Archeological Museum and the Ethnographical Museum, which originally seems to have been a temple dedicated to Serapis and then converted by the Byzantines into a basilica. On the Acropolis there are ruins of numerous monuments, the celebrated library, which once held 200,000 volumes, the sanctuary Athens, an impressive theatre, the temples of Trajan and of Dionysos, the remains of the upper agora, the monumental altar of Zeus, the sanctuary of Demeter, the Temple of Hera, the gymnasium situated on three terraces, and the lower agora.

MANISA

Manisa is a city with several examples of Seljuk and Ottoman Turkish architecture. The oldest mosque is the 14th centure Ulu Camii built by Ilyas Bey, the regional governor. The early 16th century Sultan Camii was built by Ayse Sultan, the mother of Suleyman the Magnificent. Here, every April, in the grounds of this mosque there is a Spiced Candy Festival. The 16th century Muradiye Camii was built by the architect Sinan. The medresse of this mosque today houses the Archeological Museum.

South of Manisa is the Sipildagi National Park, and nearby the famous 'crying rock' of Niobe. At Sart (Sardis) are the ruins of the ancient Sardis, the capital of the Lydian realm of Croesus on the borders of the famous river Pactole. There are the remains of the Temple of Artemis and a restored gymnasium which testify to the past splendour of this ancient city.

One of the spectacular points of the BOZDAG MOUNTAINS is the mountain village of the same name, and the Golcuk Lake. This lake is located high in the hills at an altitude of 800 m and completes the panorama. This area is a popular summer resort with its hotels and restaurants, and there are several mountain huts which can be rented. On the way down from the plateau, in Birgi, is the Cakir Aga Mansion, the wall paintings and wood used in decoration are typical Turkish architecture of the region.

SEVEN CHURCHES OF THE APOCALYPSE

The seven churches mentioned by St. John in the book of Revelation are all found in Turkey, and each was a separate community. They are Izmir (Smyrna), Efes (Ephesus), Eskihisar (Laodicea), Alasehir (Philadelphia), Sart (Sardis), Akhisar (Thyatira) and Bergama (Pergamum). Some of the sites are in a better state of preservation than others, and so tours of 1-4 days are arranged to see several or all of the 7 churches.

ÇEŞME

Cesme is 80km from Izmir. It is a typical coastal town situated on the farthest point of a peninsula jutting into the Aegean Sea. The abundance of water and springs in the area give Cesme (spring) its name. In ancient times it was called Cysus. Romans, Byzantines and later Turks ruled this area. Cesme has been an important military and commercial centre all through its history. It is possible to see ruins from every historical period.

HOW TO GET THERE

Every hour buses leave from Konak to Cesme. A daily ferry boat service Pire-Sakiz Island (Greece)-Cesme runs in the tourist season. There is a good road between Izmir and Cesme.

ACCOMMODATION

Hotels
Tuban Cesme (H1), Ilica, Tel. 1240-1; Sirin Villa (H3), Ilica Mah. Yaygin Sok., Tel. 1021-2101; Ertan (H4), Cumhuriyet Mey 12, Tel. 6795-96.
Motel
Turban Ilica, Dereboyu Mevkii Boyalik, Tel. 2128-2183.

TOURIST INFORMATION OFFICE

Iskele Meydani 6, TEL. 6653

CITY EXCURSIONS

The Cesme castle was built by the Genoese in the 14th century, and expanded and a tower added by Sultan Beyazit II in 1508. The south gate is typical Ottoman architecture. This castle was used not only as a commerical centre but also as a naval base. On the front side of the castle by the west gate is a statue to the famous admiral of Ottoman times Gazi Hasan Pasa,

Suleyman the Magnificent built a caravanserai south of the castle in 1529. This two storey U-shaped caravanserai had a large central courtyard surrounded by shops. It has been renovated and is now one of the most beautiful hotels of the area.

The Haci Memis Mosque and the Haci Mehmet Mosque are from the 18th century as are most of the mosques of Cesme. Various fountains and mausoleums are from Ottoman times.

The annual Cesme Song Contest is held in the castle. Every

year the Cesme Sea Festival is held during the first week of July. The national and international bands and folklore groups in their colourful costumes put on a good show for an enthusiastic crowd. Typical carnival games and music, plus the taverns of Cesme complete the festival-like atmosphere. The many shops and boutiques offer all kinds of arts and crafts, carpets, jewellery, leather and embroidery goods.

SURROUNDING ATTRACTIONS
ILICA

Ilica is in walking distance of Cesme on the Izmir road. It is a favourite place with the tourists because of its baths and white sandy beaches. The hot springs have been used since antiquity. For those who would like to go fishing Ilica has quite a variety. The long sunny summers give ample opportunity to those who like sun bathing and water sports. Moderately priced hotels, motels, pansiyons and restaurants are easily available.

The geographical position of Ilica makes it a centre of tourism. The thermal station Sifne, Pasa Limani, Buyuk Limani, Boyalik Koyu, the holiday complex of Altin Yunus, Ertan Beach, Dalyan, Sakizl Koyu, the village of Ciftlik and Pirlanta Beach, Altinkum Beach, Tursite Beach and the Catal Azmak Beach, situated around Ilica and Cesme, are especially attractive to the tourist.

DAYLAN

Daylan is a yacht berthing place. The amateur yachtsman will find this an ideal place with its steady afternoon breeze (Imbat) from the north-west. The Altin Yunus Marina and Leisure Centre furnishes all the necessities for an excellent yachting holiday.

ILDIN (Erythral)

Ildin is one of the twelve Ionian cities 22km north-east of Cesme. It was an important harbour. From the acropolis there is a magnificent view of Ildin Bay and the islands. The Ildin area is an ideal place for the naturalist, thanks to its wide beaches and camping possibilities.

ESEK

A surprise awaits the visitor to Esek (Donkey) Island, a short trip by sea to the north-west of Ildin. There are hundreds of donkeys running free and wild on the island.

URLA (Klazomenai)

Urla is 36km from Izmir. This is where the first civilisations of the Aegean region began. There are historical ruins of several different periods, a wealth of monuments and many thermal baths and hot springs. The Izmir Archeological Museum houses the discoveries from the excavations in the area.

SIGACIK

45km from Izmir in the Seferihisar region, Sigacik is the site of the first Turkish settlement in the Aegean. From Ottoman times and of importance are the Sigacik Mosque, Ulamis Mosque, Duzce theological school and the Sigacik bath. The fortress near the marina was built by the Genoese in the 14th century and restored by the Seljuks and Ottomans.

The Sigacik Marina is a central Aegean yachting centre. In easy walking distance from the marina is the ancient city of Teos in a delightful setting amongst olive groves. Here the ruins of the Dionysus Temple of the 2nd century BC, the theatre and the odeon are of interest. Following the asphalt road around the Sigacik Peninsula to Teos, you pass through some excellent scenery with panoramas of the village and marina, the Sigacik Pine Park and the popular Akkum Beach.

AHMETBEYLI

At the ancient city of Claros, 50km from Izmir, and today called Ahmetbeyli, is the Apollo temple. The remains of the temple and massive statues are impressive even in ruins. After seeing this site the tourist will have completed his tour and can say farewell to this lovely peninsula.

KUŞADASI (Bird Island)

Kusadasi, the ancient harbour of Skalanova, is about 90km from the city of Izmir on Turkey's Aegean coast. Built on the shores of a glittering bay around a tiny islet covered with flowers, it is a holiday maker's paradise, and one of the major gates of seaborne tourism in Turkey.

HOW TO GET THERE

By air, to Izmir airport and then by bus. Buses run from most major cities. By boat from Samos between May and October and cruises from all over the Mediterranean year round.

ACCOMMODATION

Hotels–Imbat (H2), Kadinlar Denizi, Tel. 2000-4; Akman (H3), Istikal Cad. 13, Tel. 1501-2; Marti (H3), Kadinlar Denizi, Tel. 3650-52; Stella (H3), Bezirgan Sok. 44, Tel. 1632; Aran Oteli, Kaya Aldogan Sok, Tel. 1076-1325.

Motels–Akdeniz Moteli, Karaova Mevkil, Tel. 1521-2; Omer Moteli, Yavansu Mevkil, Tel. 1017-6361.

TOURIST INFORMATION OFFICE

Iskele Meydani, Tel. 1103

CITY EXCURSIONS

Tourists are drawn here not only by the sun and sea but also by its ancient Mehmet Pasha Caravanserai (now a hotel and restaurant), its white minarets, its shady terraces where one can sit, eat grilled fish and try the many tempting bargains of its shops and boutiques. After a long day of excursions around the many sites of the region–Selcuk, Efes, Priene, Milet and Didim–Kusadasi provides the ideal atmosphere for relaxing in the restaurants that line the Kordon Promenade and the harbour entrance, enjoying a meal and a glass of excellent Turkish wine.

Kusadasi possesses one of the best equipped yacht marinas in Turkey; the Kusadasi Marina (Tel. 1752-53-54) an excellent facility with a 600 yacht capacity and all services provided including wintering both afloat and ashore.

Kusadasi is famous too, as a shopping centre with its abundance of shops and stores. Most popular is the colourful jewellery from simple coloured beads and bangles to the most sophisticated of settings in gold and silver. Well known too is the leather-ware of Kusadasi, always at very reasonable prices, and of course, carpets and rugs.

The Turkish Pop Music Festival is held here every July.

Just offshore, to the west of the town, is the small island of Guvercin Adasi (Pigeon Island) where a 14th century castle of Turkish origin now houses a cafeteria in a garden setting. For those with the time, a visit to the Dilek National Park near Kusadasi is a must. Here amidst incredibly beautiful surroundings are some of the most wonderful views and some of the rarest wild animals in Turkey-the Anatolian Cheetah, and some of Turkey's last wild horses. The park is now a wildlife preserve and a haven for several species of mammals and birds.

SURROUNDING ATTRACTIONS

Ancient sites south of Kusadasi:

PRIENE

Priene was one of the most active ports of the Ionian Federation. Making the site of particular interest is the system of geometric planning introduced in the 4th century BC by Hippodamos of Milet. The theatre is the most interesting monument of Priene. The lower tiers remain and the whole theatre preserves its interesting character. Only a few columns remain of the Temple of Athena which was a classic example of Ionian architecture. The best preserved monuments are the bouleterion (city hall) and the lower gymnasium.

MILET

This was a great Ionian port and the native city of several philosophers and sages. The theatre, reconstructed in the Roman period is an impressive building (140m of facade) built against the slope of a hill. The cavea could seat an audience of about 15,000 and most of the tiers are still intact. The theatre itself justifies a visit. The ruins of the Faustina Baths are well preserved.

DIDIM

Didim possesses only a single monument, but it is nevertheless a marvellous site. The Temple of Apollo was one of the most sacred places of antiquity. Many times looted and burned, the sanctuary is still impressive. The colossal temple (measuring 110m by 51m) was surrounded by a portico of double colonnades.

The columns that remain standing allow one to visualise the full magnitude of the building.

ALTINKUM

A holiday town 3km from Didim, with golden sand, good fish restaurants and tasty wine, this is a good place for sailing, swimming and relaxing.

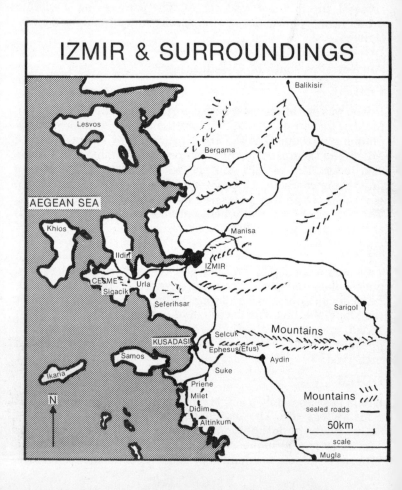

Dogu Beyazit, Ishak Pasa Mosque

Ephesus near Selcum

Sard

Pamukkale near Denizli

DENIZLI, PAMUKKALE AND ENVIRONS

Nestled against high mountains near the Buyuk Menderes River is the city of Denizli. Surrounded by the natural beauty of this verdant valley, the area is also rich in its cultural and historical remains. The Luvians were the first inhabitants, then later the Hittites occupied the area. It is no wonder this fertile plain became the site of a number of civilisations: the Frigians, Lydians, Persians, Macedonians, Romans, Byzantines, Seljuks and the Ottoman Empire. The Denizli of today is a modern city of wide streets, parks and hotels. The Ataturk Ethnographical Museum, in the city centre, is worth a visit for its folk art displays. Take your choice of the Camlik, the Incilipinar or the

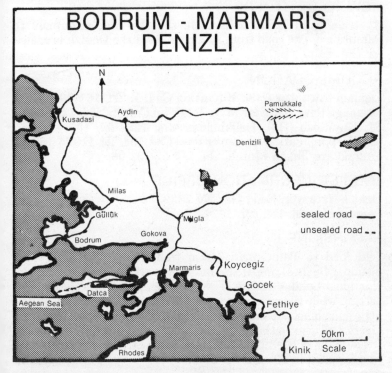

BODRUM - MARMARIS DENIZLI

N

Kusadasi
Aydin
Pamukkale
Denizili
Milas
Güllük
Mugla
Gokova
Bodrum
Marmaris
Koycegiz
Gocek
Datca
Aegean Sea
Fethiye
Rhodes
Kinik

sealed road
unsealed road

50km
Scale

Gokpinar parks in which to rest, picnic or walk through the forest in the shade of the pine trees. The fresh water springs and thermal baths have attracted many visitors. Industrially, weaving and agriculture are important.

PAMUKKALE

Pamukkale is an extraordinary natural wonder. The calceous waters come out of the ground at a temperature of 35°C and tumble down the mountain side from a height of 100m, forming myriads of pools. Cotton-coloured stalactites are formed as the water overflows the pools, creating a breath-taking sight unequalled in the world. Water is the sole architect of this gleaming fairy-castle resembling cotton or snow, and hence its name 'Cotton Castle'. In this wonderland are hot springs in abundance which are recommended for the treatment of heart diseases, circulatory problems, high blood pressure, nervous disorders, rheumatism and eye and skin diseases.

HOW TO GET THERE

By train from Izmir to Denizli, then by bus or dolmus to Pamukkale. The road from Izmir via Aydin to Denizli is sealed for the entire length.

ACCOMMODATION

Denizili–Altuntur (H3), Kaymakci Cad. 1, Tel. 161 76-166 93; Etemaga (H4), Saraylar Mah, Istasyon Cad. 34, Tel. 145 68-138 51; Kuyumcu (H4), Deliklicinar Mey 128, Tel. 137 49-50-53 (US$10 ppn); Park (H4), Enver Pasa Cad. 104, Tel. 119 17-150 47. Pamukkate–Tusan Moteli, Tel. 214 32-132 06.

TOURIST INFORMATION OFFICE

Denizli–Istasyon Cad., Gar Tel 13393
Pamukkale, Tel. Denizli, 1077.

EXCURSIONS

The road to Pamukkale, 19km from Denizli, is lined with oleander bushes, preparing one for the relaxing atmosphere of this ideal holiday centre. The hotel pools are in a garden-like setting while the natural ones on the hillside outside, with their little splashing waterfalls, are particularly appreciated by sports lovers and sun bathers.

The ruins of Hierapolis are the other main attraction. The city was founded in 190 BC by Eumenes 11, king of Pergamon. In the 2nd and 3rd centuries it reached the high point in its development as a Roman thermal bath centre. Hierapolis has such extensive ruins that the following touristic route is suggested. After taking note of the city walls, start with the octagonal Martyrium of St. Philip. Cross over to the 2nd century theatre to see some fine marble reliefs above the stage, all quite well preserved. Next to the Temple of Apollo is a holy area. A deep hole in the ground (Plutonium) used to emit noxious fumes (carbon dioxide) which the priests said were fatal to all except themselves. A monumental fountain is nearby. In the pool of the Pamukkale Motel are large marble slabs belonging to a Roman bath. Then go to the basilica, up a colonnaded street, through memorial gates from Byzantine and Roman times and to the West Bath, ending up at the necropolis. This necropolis area stretches for 2km and contains some of the best examples of tomb styles, and is one of the best preserved cemeteries in all of Turkey. The now restored East Bath is an archeological museum housing many of the remains from Hierapolis.

The few shops in Pamukkale offer various calcified objects unique to this area. Bottles are particularly sought after. Rugs and kilims from the locality are also available. In contrast to this very white background, the annual June Pamukkale Festival seems even more colourful. Tours to other places of interest in the area are made from Pamukkale.

SURROUNDING ATTRACTIONS

KARAHAYIT is another thermal centre 5km north-west from Pamukkale where the water has a high iron content. Photographs taken here have an interesting variation because of the red tones from the earth. There are some other thermal baths and camping grounds in this area.

AKHAN is the site of a 13th century Seljuk caravanserai. The mosque inside the caravanserai and the inscriptions over the doors are of the same period. One side is overlaid with white marble, hence its name 'White Inn'. Akhan is 17km from Pamukkale and 8km from Denizli on the Ankara road.

ESKIHISAR-LAODICEA. In the upper valley of the Buyuk Mendered River, near Eskihisar, is the ancient city of Laodicea, 17km from Pamukkale and 8km from Denizli. The Selecuid ruler Antiochos II rebuilt the city in the 3rd century BC and named it after his wife. Like Ephesus and Miletos, Laodicea was on the main trade route to Syria and Mesopotamia. It is one of the seven churches of the Apocalypse. Even though Byzantines, Seljuks (1095) and Ottomans (1390) occupied the city, the ruins to be seen today-a theatre, gymnasium, aqueducts, walls, a church and a stadium-are mainly Roman. The ruins are not the only attraction; there is also the view across the valley to Pamukkale.

BULDAN is a lovely site famous for its use of a gold-like thread in decorative embroidery work on cloth. The various items are attractively priced. With its little weaving workshops and the colourful, friendly shopping areas, Buldan is in a world of its own.

GEYRE-APHRODISIAS. The history of this city goes back a long way, but the important part of the city was built in the 1st century BC. Some of the richest art finds have come from the excavations of this city that was dedicated to Aphrodite, the goddess of love and fertility. The buildings are adorned with marble that was carved with skill, producing remarkable temples, monuments, theatres, baths and a magnificent stadium. Their reputation for the exquisite finesse of their statuary and marble craftmanship soon spread to other parts of the then known world. It thus became the centre of the greatest sculpturing school of antiquity. A highlight of any visit is the marvellous remains now housed in the museum.

BODRUM

Bodrum is a town of white houses hung with flowers, rising tier upon tier against a green hill overlooking a dazzling blue bay, guarded by the great medieval castle built by the Knights of Rhodes.

HOW TO GET THERE

By Plane to Izmir or Dalaman Airports, from there, regular bus services to Bodrum.

By road, Bodrum is serviced by road connections to major centres.

By sea, ferry boat service (daily from May to October) from the Greek Island of Kos (Istankoy), cruises from all over the Mediterranean.

ACCOMMODATION

Hotels-Baraz (H3), Cumhuriyet Cad. 58, Tel. 1857; Gozen (H3), Cumhuriyet Cad. 18, Tel 1602; Gala (H4), Nayzen Tevfik Cad., Tel. 2216; Mercam (H4), Ataturk Cad. 103, Tel. 2670 (package tours are available from England to this hotel – £236 for 7 nights, £275 for 14 nights including air fares).

Motels-Halikarnas, Cumhuriyet Cad. 128, Tel. 1073; Regal, Bitez Yalisi, Tel. Kabakum 58,; TMT, Akcebuk, Tel. 1440-3, Kaktus, Ortakent, Tel. 10.

Guest Houses-Artemis, Cumhuriyet Cad. 117, Tel. 2530; Feslegen, Cumhuriyet Cad. Papatya Sox, 18/1, Tel. 2910; Cem, Uckuyular Cad. 13, Tel. 1757; Heredot, Neyzen Tevfik Cad. 116, Tel. 93 (package tours are available from England to this motel – £226 for 7 nights, £259 for 14 nights including air fares); Manzara, Kumbahce Mah, Meteoroloji Yani, Tel. 1719. Camping-yaz, Gumbet, Tel. 174.

TOURIST INFORMATION OFFICE

12 Eylul Meydani, Tel. 1091.

EXCURSIONS

Bodrum, the birthplace of Herodotus, where the Mediterranean and the Aegean meet, about 200 km. from Dalaman airport, is one of the most beautiful holiday resorts in Turkey, with its long waterfront shaded by palm trees.

In ancient times it was known as Halicarnassus, where the Tomb of King Mausolus was one of the Seven Wonders of the World. Excavations are now bringing the remains of this to light, and on the site is the Mausoleum Museum. The Castle of St. Peter is one of the region's finest examples of architecture and well worth a visit. In the castle, too, is an interesting museum of antiquities brought up from the seabed. On nearby Goktepe is a 10,000 seat theatre built in the 2nd century AD.

Special to Bodrum is the lively, friendly and bohemian atmosphere. Indeed, Bodrum is the meeting place of the art community of Turkey and has many small galleries. There is a variety of night life to suit your every desire, dancing the night away in one of the lively discotheques, or just relaxing over a glass of Aegean wine.

Every year the Bodrum Arts and Culture Festival is held here.

Shopping is a delight in Bodrum. Leather goods of all kinds, natural sponges, and the local blue beads are among the bargains to be found in the many friendly little shops along the narrow white-walled streets. Here you will find woven rugs, carpets, embroidery and copper. Also, try the lovely and original leisure clothes in soft cotton.

Along the shore there are many fine sandy beaches, easily accessible by road, or arrange a group and hire a boat and explore the quiet coves and wooded islands of this beautiful peninsula. Inland, little windmills still used to grind grain crown hills covered with olive groves.

The fine new coast road will assist you in exploring this lovely region. If you do not have your car with you, there are frequent minibuses serving all the villages and beaches.

SURROUNDING ATTRACTIONS

North of Bodrum are the enchanting little fishing villages of TURKBUKU, TORBALI and GULLUK. Near Gulluk at Varvil is the ancient site of Bargilya with the remains of ramparts and a threatre, and the ruins of some Byzantine churches.

Inland to the north, the town of MILAS is renowned for its handmade carpets, and visitors may watch the craftsmen knotting them. In this town there are many fine examples of old Turkish houses with carved timbers and latticed windows.

The road westward from Bodrum at TURGUTREIS passes through many citrus orchards. This region is famous for oranges, mandarines and lemons. In the hedges pomegranates and bay laurels grow wild. And with its mild climate and gentle sea air, the whole peninsula is colourful with flowers in every season.

Turgutreis, birthplace of the great Turkish admiral of that name, and GUMUSLUK, the ancient port of Myndos, are two small harbours on the west coast of the peninsula.

KARAADA, Black Island, lies 8km off the shore from Bodrum. Take a boat trip to bathe in the grotto where the warm mineral waters flowing out of the rocks are believed to beautify the complexion.

The GULF OF GOKOVA, along the south shore of the peninsula, is a very deep and beautiful gulf with thickly wooded shores. The colours of the translucent waters must be seen to be believed, varying from deepest blue to palest turquoise, and in the evenings they reflect the mountains silhouetted by the setting sun. At night these waters are often phosphorescent. You can take a boat from Bodrum for a two, three or seven day tour or more of the gulf, which will give you one of your most wonderful memories of your holiday at Bodrum.

MARMARIS–DATÇA–FETHIYE

HOW TO GET THERE

By plane–from Istanbul or Ankara to Dalaman airport, from there by bus.

By bus–regular dolmus (minibus) services to Fethiye, Koycegiz, Marmaris and Datca from Izmir and Bodrum.

By sea–from Rhodes to Marmaris. From Symi to Datca. Turkish Maritime Lines runs a service in season to this area. Group tours may be arranged for the fabulous 'Blue Voyage' tours, prices vary according to season.

ACCOMMODATION

Marmaris

Hotels–Yavuz (H2), Ataturk Cad., Tel. 2937-38; Atlantik (H3), Ataturk Cad. 34, Tel. 1218-1236; Lidya (H3), Siteler Mah. 130, Tel. 2940-2; Orkide (H3), Siteler Mah., Tel. 2580 (package tours are available from England to this hotel – £279 for 7 nights, £365 for 14 nights including air fares); Otel 47 (H3), Ataturk Cad. 10, Tel. 1700-2730; Karadeniz (H4), Ataturk Bul., Tel. 1064; Marmaris (H4), Ataturk Bul. 30, Tel. 1308-1173; Murat (H4), Kenan Evren Bul., Tel. 1850.

Camping–Amazon Kamp, Hisar Onu Koyu; Aktur Kamping Tatil Sitesi, Emecik Koyu, Tel. 106; Deniz Kamp, Oludeniz Fethiye, Tel. 8-12.

Datca

Fudayali (H3), Iskele Cad., Tel. 1042; Dorya Moteli, Iskele Mah., Tel. 35-36; Aydi Tur Moteli, Resadiye Mah., Karakesit Mevkii, Tel. 2343-53.

Fethiye

Dedeoglu (H4), Iskele Mey, Tel. 1606-1707 (package tours are available from England to this hotel – £252 for 7 nights, £309 for 14 nights including air fares); Likya (H4), Karagozler Mah., Tel. 1169-1690; Mutlu (H4), Calis, Mevkii, Sahilyolu, (package tours, as above, £248 for 7 nights, £306 for 14 nights); Meri Moteli, Oludeniz, Tel. Oludeniz 1; Seketur Moteli, Calis Gullukbasi, Tel. 1705-1015

TOURIST INFORMATION OFFICES
Marmaris-Iskele Meydani 39, Tel. 1035
Datca-Iskele Mah, Belediye Binasi, Tel. 1163
Fethiye-Iskele Meydani 1, Tel. 1527
Dalaman-Dalaman Havaalani, Tel. 1220
Koycegiz-Kordon-Golpark 1, Tel. 1703

MARMARIS.
Marmaris, where the Aegean meets the Mediterranean, is one of the most beautiful holiday areas in Turkey. Here pine forests stretch down to the shores of an immense bay dotted with tiny islands, bringing cooling breezes even in the heat of summer.

Marmaris has everything for all members of the family. Alongside the old fishing port is the modern yacht marina. All along the shores of the almost landlocked bay are beaches of golden sand. The clear calm sea is warm enough for swimming from early June to late September. You can find here fine modern hotels, simple restaurants and cafes in quiet coves. Elsewhere lively discotheques are located by the shore, and the safe bathing makes this an ideal spot for children's holidays. The Marmaris Festival in June offers a colourful mixture of art, culture and music.

Like all the Aegean and Mediterranean coastline, Marmaris is richly adorned with history as well as bewildering nature. Marmaris itself, was the ancient Physkos, an important stop on the Anatolian-Rhodes-Egypt trade route. Marmaris contains little now to remind us of this impressive past; a 16th century citadel, a bridge and a caravanserai, but around the bay surrounding the city are some impressive ruins.

At Kumlubuku, reached by boat from Marmaris, is the ancient city of Amos on the northern side of the bay, where there are remains of a temple and a theatre. At the tip of the Bozburun Peninsula, also reachable by boat, is Loryma, where ruins of the ancient harbour and castle can be seen. Sidera Island in the Gulf of Gokova, the ancient Cedrai, can be visited by car to Gelibolu Bay then by boat. On this island are the old city walls, a theatre, temples and a sandy beach. Boats ferry passengers to and from the hotels around the great bay. Or hire a boat yourself (your hotel will help you) and explore the many islands in the bay and picnic and swim from a beach that is all your own.

DATCA.

Make an excursion to Datca (76km from Marmaris) a
picturesque holiday town perched up above the sea, with a
splendid beach of sand nearby. All along the peninsula on the
way to Datca the road winds among trees with views over the
deep blue sea. A tourist will not be bored in this town with
plenty of entertainment, bars, cafes, discotheques and shops.
Yachters will find a marina and will want to make this a stopover.
The white houses of this town make it a typical Mediterranean
setting. Go right to the end of the peninsula to visit the ruins
of the ancient Carian city of Knidos, once famous as a centre
of art and culture in the 4th-6th centuries BC. On a headland
looking over the sea are the remains of two theatres and a
circular temple dedicated to Aphrodite.

Along the road to Fethiye the Gokova Park is a sure choice
for those who need a rest from the sun. Make a stop at the town
of Koycegiz, beside a lake of the same name. From Dalyan you
can rent a small boat and explore all the maze of waterways
through a marshland leading to the sea, beaches and fresh fish
restaurants. Opposite Dalyan are the ruins of the ancient city
of Caunos with its vast theatre that could seat 15,000 people,
and tombs cut in the cliff.

FETHIYE

Fethiye, 135km east from Marmaris is one of the most beautiful
marina parklands and overlooks a bay strewn with islands. The
houses look down on the little port from a hill crowned by the
ruins of the fortress built by the Knights of Rhodes.

Across the bay from Fethiye, the bay of Gocek dotted with
islands and indented with hundreds of bays, is irresistible to a
yachtsman. Arymaxa is one of the most famous of the ancient
cities, especially the baths near the water; and on Tersane Island
are Byzantine ruins including one of their shipyards.

Renting a boat is the best way to explore the Belcegiz Bay,
the beautiful Olu Deniz, a calm lagoon of crystal clear water,
ideal for swimming and sailing, with pine forests along its shores
and the Gemiler Island covered with Byzantine ruins. Kidirak
is a private beach with a shady park. For those who prefer
camping the Belcegiz Beach is the recommended site. Katranci
is a park of similar quality reached by road or sea.

At Fethiye, the ancient Telmessos, there are numerous Lycian
rock tombs cut out of the cliff face, with carved facades

reproducing the buildings of those far off times. The most remarkable is that known now as the Tomb of Amyntas, which probably dates from the 4th century BC. Its facade has two Ionic columns, over which there is a pediment above a frieze. The tomb chamber is reached through a small opening which can be closed by a movable slab of stone.

About 65km from Fethiye, near Kinik, are the ruins of Xanthos, an ancient city whose history goes back to before the 8th century BC. Excavations have uncovered the Lycian and Romans acropolis, and much of the theatre is still well preserved. There are also many inscribed sarcophagi and monuments.

At Letoon, near Xanthos, there are three temples dedicated to Leto, Artemis and Apollo.

Wandering among remarkable ruins of ancient times, sailing in a fresh breeze over the blue waves, just lazing idly on a beach of golden sand. . .however you dream of spending your holiday, you will find what you are looking for on this loveliest stretch of the Turkish Coast.

THE TURQUOISE COAST
(The Turkish Riviera)

The majestic Toros (Taurus) Mountains plunge down to a Mediterranean edged by a narrow luxuriant coastal belt covered in wild oleanders, orange and lemon groves, pine forests and palm trees, date and banana plantations. The intensely colourful region is bathed in sunshine for 300 days a year, and clear turquoise waters, secluded coves, rocky headlands and broad bays fringed by sandy beaches are ideal for swimming, sailing,and all water sports. It is one of the rare regions in the world where, in March and April, it is possible to ski in the snowy Toros Mountains in the mornings then bathe in the warm waters of the Mediterranean in the afternoons. The coast is rich in legend and history, with many great ruins of ancient cities and theatres, and great Crusader castles. In classical time Lycia lay to the west; the great Pamphylian cities of Perge and Aspendos were between present-day Antalya and Side. Mark Anthony gave the lovely Cilician shores to Cleopatra as a wedding gift.

HOW TO GET THERE

By road–A good asphalt road from Antalya to Mersin links the resorts of this 500km long coastline, and the region is well connected by road to the rest of the country.

By sea–In summer the Turkish Maritime Lines operate a regular service from Istanbul to this coastal region and back, with the liners calling at all main resorts.

By plane–Turkish Airlines operate daily flights from Istanbul to Antalya and Adana.

ACCOMMODATION

Adana

Hotels–Divan (HL), Inonu Cad. 142, Tel. 22701-4; Buyuk Surmeli (HL), Ozler Cad., Tel. 21944-5, Inci (H3), Kurtulus Cad., Tel. 22612; Ipek Palas (H3), Inonu Cad. 103, Tel. 18743-5; Koza (H3), Ozler Cad. 103, Tel. 18853; Atto-tr-Set (H3), Inonu Cad. 40, Tel. 13031; Santral Palas (H3), Abidinpasa Cad. 60, Tel. 18715; Agba (H4), Abidinpasa Cad. 1/A, Tel. 22459; Duygu (H4),

Inonu Cad. 14, Tel. 16741; Erciyes Palas (H4), Ozler Cad. 53, Tel. 18867-69.
Camping-Rasit Ener, 3km from Adana on the Iskenderun Road, Tel. 11904.

Antalya
Hotels-Talya (HL), Fevzi Cakmak Cad., Tel. 15600-9; Olimpos (H2), Kemer Nahiyesi, Tel. 29-33; Bilgehan (H3), Kazim Ozalp Cad. 194, Tel. 15184 (US$65 ppn); Kemer Doruk (H3), Tel. Kemer 1125-1358; Lara (H3), Lara Yolu PK 404, Tel., 15299; Buyuk (H4), Cumhuriyet Cad. 57, Tel. 11499; Perge (H4), Parkici Perge Sok 5, Tel. 23600-11432; Tataoglu (H4), Kazim Ozalp Cad. 91, Tel. 12119; Yalcim (H4), Husnu Karakas Cad. 1253 Sok, Tel. 14190; Yaylapalas (H4), Ali Cetinkaya Cad. 12, Tel. 11913-14.
Holiday Village-Guneydeniz Mevklii, Camyuva Koyu
Camping-Kervansaray Mokamp-Alanya 110km; Camping Turban Kiziltepe-Kemer, Tel. 113.

Alanya
Hotels-Alantur (h1), Camyolu Koyu, Tel. 1224; Alaaddin (H2), Saray Mah, Tel. 2624 (US$25 ppn); Alara (H2), Yesilkoy, Tel. 46; Alanya Buyuk (H3), Guller Pinan Mah, Tel. 1138; Banana (H3), Cikcikli Koyu, Tel. 1548; Bayirli (H3), Iskele Cad., Tel. 1487; Kaptan (H3), Iskele Cad. 62, Tel. 2000; Berrin (H4), Guller Pinan Mah, Tel. 2830; Cimen (H4), Guller Pinari Mah, Gazi Pasa Cad., Tel. 2283; Gunaydin (H4), Kultur Cad. 30, Tel. 1943; Kleopatra (H4), Saray Mah, Tel. 13980; Mesut (H4), Obakoy Gol Mevkii, Tel. 1339; Ozen (H4), Muftuler Cad. 38, Tel. 2220, Park (H4), Hurriyet Meyd, Tel. 1675; Pehlivan (H4) Saray Mah. Kalearkasi, Tel. 2781.
Motels-Alan tur, Camyolu Koyu, Tel. 1224; Turtas, Serapsu Mevkii, Konakli Koyu, Tel. Konakli 1; Comertoglu, Avsaliar Koyu, Tel. 721; Merhaba, Keykubat Cad. Tel. 1251; Panorama, Guller Pinari Mah., Tel. 1181; Yeni Motel International, Keykubat Cad., Tel. 1195.

Antakya
Hotels-Atahan (H2), Hurriyet Cad. 28, Tel. 11036; Divan (H3), Istikial Cad. 62, Tel. 11518

Mersin
Hotels-Mersin (H1), Camii Serif Mah. 10. Sok. 2, Tel. 12200; Atlihan (H2), Istikial Cad., Tel. 24153-58; Toros (H3), Ataturk Cad. 33, Tel. 12201; Sahil Marti (H3), Viranseir Mah, Mezitli,

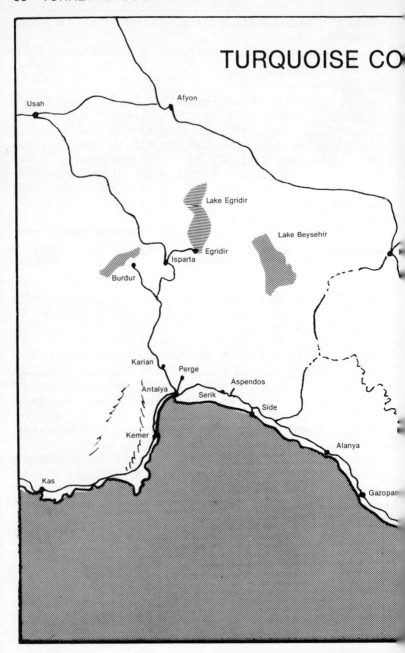

TURQUOISE CO

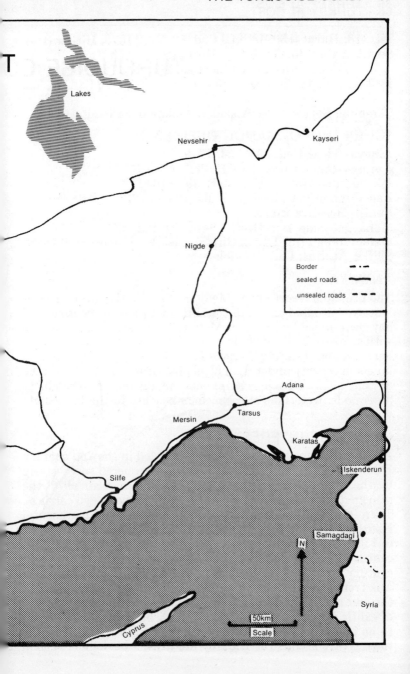

Tel. 318; Hayat (H4), Istiklal Cad. 88, Tel. 11076; Hititer (H4),
Soguksu Cad. 40, Tel. 16327; Hosta (H4), Fasih Kayabali Cad.
4, Tel. 14760; Nobel (H4), Istiklai Cad. 123, Tel. 11227; Ocak (H4),
Istiklal Cad. 48, Tel. 15765; Savran (H4), Soguksu Cad. 46, Tel.
11505.
Camping-Kervansaray Kizkalesi Mokamp-Erdemli, P.K. 7.

TOURIST INFORMATION OFFICES

Alanya-Iskele Cad. 56/6, Tel. 1240
Antalya-Cumhuriyet Cad. 91, Tel. 11747-15271
Iskenderun-Ataturk Bul. 49/B, Tel. 11640
Kas-Cumhuriyet Meydani 6, Tel. 1238-3226
Kemer-Belediye Binasi
Manavgat-Side Yolu Uzeri 1.5km, Tel. Side 265
Mersin-Inonu Bul. Liman Giris Sahasi, Tel. 11265-12710-16358
Silifke-Ataturk Cad. 1/2, Tel. 1151

ANTALYA

The principal resort of the Mediterranean is the lovely port of
Antalya, situated on top of the cliffs of a wide crescent-shaped
bay surrounded by the Toros Mountains. It is an attractive city
with shady palm-lined boulevards, picturesque old quarters and
harbour, and the lovely Pergole Park. There are several modern
hotels in the city and it is an ideal place from which to visit the
ancient sites of Lycia, Pamphylia and Pisidia and the shady
pinewoods, waterfalls and spacious beaches in the immediate
vicinity.

PLACES OF INTEREST

Antalya, the ancient Attaleia, was founded in the 2nd century
BC by Attalus II of Pergamon and was conquered successively
by the Romans and Seljuks. It is possible to visit all of the
principal monuments either on foot or by horse-drawn carriage.
There are well preserved city ramparts and the monumental
Hadrian's Gate, in beautifully decorated marble, which was built
in 130 AD. The region was occupied by the Seljuks in the 13th
century and was joined to the Ottoman Empire in the 14th
century. Nearby is the Kesik Minare (truncated minaret) which
was transformed from a Byzantine church into a mosque. At
the end of the Pergole Park, which boasts an amazing variety
of exotic flowers and plants is the Hidirlik Kulesi, which used
to be an old lighthouse. Along the road from the park to the
town centre stands the Karatay Medresse (theological school)

Kiz Kalesi near Mersin

Cappadocia

Konya, Whirling Dervishes

Ankara, Mausoleum of Ataturk

Houses in Sanfranbolu

Istanbul, Belly Dancer

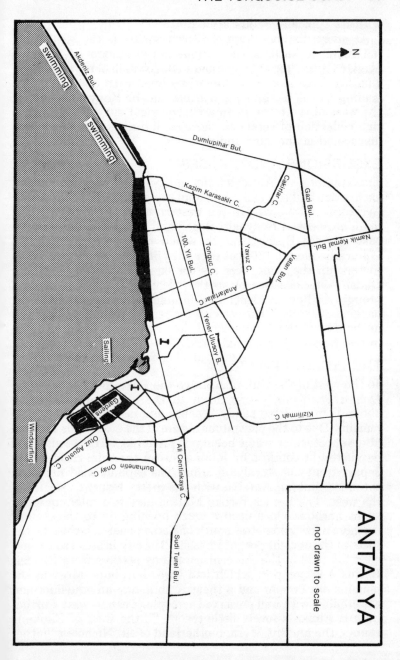

with its typically Seljuk style portal.

At short distance from the town square is the identifying landmark of Antalya, the curious fluted minaret of the Yivli Minare Cami. From here one can walk downhill along the narrow winding streets of the old quarters lined with wooden houses leading to the picturesque marina. On the Konyaalti road, at the west of the town, is an archaeological museum housing a rich collection of ceramics, mosaics, figurines and sarcophagi discovered in the surrounding areas.

EXCURSIONS AND CRUISES

The environs of Antalya offer many possibilities for short excursions and one can join a mini-cruise and visit the ancient Lycian sites by boat. On the western edge of the town is the hugh crescent of Konyaalti Beach and a short distance to the east is Lara Beach near to which the spectacular Duden Waterfalls plunge 150 feet over the cliff edge to the sea, while further up the same river are the equally spectacular Upper Duden Waterfalls. Nearby are the paleolithic Karain Caves which brought to light evidence of a human settlement from as far back as 50,000BC. The old city fortress of Termessos lies high in the hills to the north-west of the town and is today situated in the Termessos National Park.

THE LYCIAN PENINSULA

To the west of the Gulf of Antalya the Toros Mountains of the Lycian Peninsula sweep down to the sea, and this region abounds in deserted sandy beaches and fascinating historical remains. Due to the precipitous nature of the mountains the road offers spectacular scenic beauty. If preferred, all of the sites can be visited in comfort by joining one of the mini-cruises that depart from the Antalya marina. The asphalt road has been extended, linking Antalya with the pretty resort of Kemer to the west. The Kemer Turban Marina here is a fully equipped yacht harbour. On a narrow creek opening on to the Gulf of Antalya a few kilometres south of Kemer, near Tekirova, lie the ruins of the ancient port of Phaselis. The city is believed to have been founded in the 7th century BC by settlers from Rhodes. It was a major port which had three harbours. Most of the remains are Roman and a theatre, an agora, an aqueduct and a necropolis with well preserved sarcophagi can be seen. Further west is Finike a lovely little resort. To the west of Finike is Demre, the ancient Myra, motherland of St. Nicholas, 'Father

Christmas', who was bishop of this Mediterranean city during the 4th century. His tomb lies in a recently restored basilica and there are impressive Lycian rock tombs and a Roman theatre behind the town. Just a short boat ride away from Demre Dalyanagzi harbour is the island of Kekova, a yachtsman's paradise, where there are Byzantine ruins and the remains of a Lycian city with partially submerged sarcophagi. The friendly village of Kas, with its bars, restaurants and guesthouses is an ideal place for holidays. It is situated at the foot of a mountain along the shores of a wide bay. In the town the remains of a small Lycian theatre and some Lycian rock tombs now standing in the sea can be seen. Further west, the pretty fishing village of Kalkan, the ancient harbour of Patara, the Lycian capital of Xanthos and the Lycian holy centre of Letoon temples can be visited.

THE LAKE DISTRICT

In the Lake District, 150km north of Antalya, renowned for its natural beauty, are several natural beaches. In the restaurants around Egridir Lake the white bass and prawns are especially popular. At the Kovada Lake in the Kovada National Park south of Egridir and at the Gulluk Lake south of Isparta are two of Turkey's most beautiful natural areas. Isparta is surrounded by rose gardens, and the cosmetic products obtained from the rose oil are eagerly purchased by tourists. Isparta which is renowned for its carpets too, has an interesting museum.

PERGE

The coast between Antalya and Alanya is intensively cultivated and indented by several streams and rivers; here was the ancient Pamphylia and the land bears the imprint of various civilisations. A turning from the main road at the village of Aksu leads to the ruins of Perge.

Just outside the city walls is a Roman theatre which could seat an audience of 15,000. The auditorium has a colonnaded gallery running around the top and was built against a hillside. Next to the theatre is an impressive stadium (234m x 34m), one of the biggest and best preserved of antiquity. The Hellenistic enclosure is entered by a Roman gate behind which lies a triumphal arch that has been restored. Further along is the older city gate, dating from the 3rd century BC, which is flanked by two lofty round towers and contains a horseshoe-shaped court. This gate leads on to a long colonnaded way that was once lined with shops and sidewalks paved in mosaic. Opposite the ruins of the large agora, which was surrounded by colonnades lined with shops, stands a 10m building which used to house the thermal baths and gymnasium.

ASPENDOS

A turning from the main road at Serik leads to the ruins of another important Pamphylian city, Aspendos, set on the banks of the ancient Eurymedon River, today called the Koprucayi.

Dominating the site is the best preserved theatre of antiquity dating from the 2nd century AD. Built partly against a hill, it could seat an audience of 15,000. 40km to the north is the Koprulu Canyon National Park which contains some ancient Roman bridges.

SIDE

This pretty resort with its local population of fishermen is surrounded by lush orange groves, banana plantations and cotton fields. A few years ago only a few wooden cottages stood near the site, but not surprisingly, the resort has become very popular in recent years as more and more travellers discover its attractions, and now there are modern hotels, motels and scores of guest houses.

The walls and towers of the ancient city are very well preserved and there is a partially extant aqueduct. Opposite the entrance, outside the city walls, is an exquisite fountain and Roman baths which now house a museum displaying statues recovered from the site. The entrance portal is flanked by two towers, and immediately upon entering is the theatre which dominates the site; it could seat an audience of 25,000 and is remarkable in that the cavea was not built on to a hill, but was constructed. Next to the theatre is the first agora, which is completely surrounded by porticoes and shops, with the ruins of a temple dedicated to Tyche in the centre. There is a second agora, and scattered throughout the rest of the site are the ruins of temples dedicated to Apollo and Artemis, a Byzantine basilica, numerous fountains and the remains of private Roman houses and a harbour.

ALANYA

The town of Alanya nestles at the foot of a rocky promontory which juts out between two sandy beaches and is crowned by a Seljuk fortress, which is one of the most impressive sights on the Mediterranean coast.

The city was founded in the 4th century BC and during Roman times was a notorious pirate stronghold. It was later annexed by the Seljuk Sultan Alaeddin Keykubat, who made Alanya his winter residence and naval base. Near the harbour are the unique arched boatyards which were built by the Seljuks, and the Kizil Kule (Red Tower) of the same period. A road, with breathtaking views at every bend, winds its way up to the citadel and passes the picturesque cottages of the old town.

The well preserved double-walled fortress has 150 towers still standing and contains ruins of mosques, a Byzantine church, a covered bazaar, a caravanserai and cisterns. Down below is a dizzy view of the rocks fringing the promontory contrasting with the brilliant turquoise waters of the Mediterranean, while from every side are magnificent views of the modern town, the harbour, the long white beaches, and the foothills of the snowcapped Toros Mountains sloping down to the sea.

At the foot of the promontory on the western side is the Damlatas Cave, small and extremely old with wonderful multi-hued stalagmites and stalactites. The humidity in the cave is very high and is said to benefit sufferers of asthma and respiratory diseases. Opposite the cave is a beach and nearby is the local archaeological and ethnographical museum. Of special interest are the Bleu Grotto, with its phosphorescent rocks, and the Kizlar Magaresi (Maidens' Cave), where the pirates used to keep their female captives.

FROM ALANYA TO SILIFKE

The road east of Alanya leads to Gazipasa, a pleasant village with a beautiful beach. After Gazipasa is the most beautiful stretch of coastline in Turkey, the road clings to the pine-clad mountain slopes which plunge steeply down to the sea offering spectacular views of cliffs, coves and the brilliant turquoise waters of the Mediterranean. Just outside Anamur are the ruins of ancient Anemorium with double ramparts, a theatre, an odeon and a necropolis. The town of Anamur nestles in the mountains a few kilometres inland. The fine, well pre-served Crusader castle is nearby, set between two curving sandy beaches, and from the top of the fort a splendid view of the surrounding countryside and coast can be seen. East of Anamur the road rises and falls until the Plain of Silifke. Just before Silifke is the little resort of Tasucu with its sandy beach and harbour from where a regular car ferry service is operated to Cyprus. Just south of Silifke is a Roman necropolis and church of Ayatekia, the first female martyr.

Located slightly inland is Silifke itself, set at the foot of a fortress crowning the hill that was the acropolis of the ancient Seleucia and Calycadnos. In the town is an old bridge crossing the ancient Calycadnos River, today called the Goksu, and the remains of a Roman theatre, temple and necropolis. In the Silifke Museum are exhibits discovered in the region. To the north is Uzuncaburc, the ancient olba-Diocaesarea, where architectural remains of the hellenistic period and the impressive remains of the Temple of Zeus Olbius can be seen.

FROM SILIFKE TO MERSIN

The road from Silifke to Mersin closely follows the coast, passing pines and orange groves, and is flanked on the one side by ruins of cities, basilicas and tombs, and on the other by a series of small secluded coves with sandy beaches.

Just beyond Silifke at the little fishing village of Narlikuyu, is a Roman mosaic depicting the Three Graces. Further on are the deep chasms known as Cennet-Cehenriem (Heaven and Hell) with the ruins of a 5th century chapel in the chasm known as Heaven. Nearby is a deep cave full of stalagmites and stalactites, believed to benefit sufferers of respiratory diseases (like the Damlatas Cave near Alanya). At the resort and ancient site of Korykos are fine sandy beaches, modern motels and camp sites. The Castle of Korykos stands next to the beach opposite another castle, Kiz kalesi (Maiden Castle) which stands on an islet 100m off shore. The two castles used to be joined by a sea wall, but that no longer exists. Near Kanlidivane are the ruins of ancient Kanytelis with tombs resembling small temples and sarcophagi dating from Roman times. Viransehir, ancient Pompetopolis, was founded in 700BC by the Rhodians, and among the remains are a row of Corinthian columns that once lined the Sacred Way.

MERSIN TARSUS

Surrounded by lush market gardens Mersin, with its shady palm-lined avenues, city park and modern hotels, is a convenient base from which to visit the nearby historical sites and numerous beaches and coves fringing the densely cultivated land. It is a rapidly developing city and the largest port on the Turkish Mediterranean, with a regular car ferry service to

Cyprus. In the Mersin fish market are several inexpensive restaurants.

To the east of Mersin on the edge of the fertile Cukurova Plain, is Tarsus, the birth-place of St. Paul, nestling in the foothills of the Taurus Mountains amid cedar groves. Of ancient origin, the city was conquered and invaded on several occasions so there are few ancient remains: the Cleopatra Gate, through which Mark Anthony and Cleopatra passed when they met each other in Tarsus, an ancient church, and the Ottoman period Ulu Cami. Another place worth visiting is a pretty spot in the outskirts of the town known as the Tarsus Falls, with little streams, waterfalls and shady trees.

ADANA

Set in the heart of the Cukurova Plain, on the banks of the River Seyhan, is Turkey's fourth largest city, Adana, the centre of a rich agricultural region and thriving cotton industry. The river is spanned by the ancient Taskopru (stone bridge), which was built by Hadrian and renovated by Justinian; only 14 of the bridge's original 21 arches are still standing. Also of interest in the city are the Akca Mescit (Chapel Mosque), the 14th century Ulu Cami, and an ancient covered bazaar. Well worth visiting is the archaeological and ethnographical museum which houses locally excavated Hittite, Assyrian, Neo-Babylonian, Hellenistic and Roman remains.

On the road from Iskenderun lies Misis, which derived its wealth from its position on the caravan route between China, Persia and the Indies. There are several Roman remains to be seen, including a beautiful mosaic of the 4th century representing Noah's Ark and the animals. Further along the road is the impressive ruins of the fortress Yilanlikake, set atop a rocky peak dominating the River Ceyhan. Between Kadirli and Kozan lies the village of Anavarza, the ancient Anazarbus, where the ruins of a Roman-Byzantine city can be seen. At the Neo-Hittite site of Karatepe are the remains of the summer residence of King Asitawada, where tablets bearing bi-lingual inscriptions were discovered. This is now the site of the Karatepe National Park and open-air museum.

ISKENDERUN

The road from Adana to Iskenderun crosses the Plain of Issos, where Alexander the Great defeated Dairus III and the Persian Army in 333 BC. A still impressive fortress at Toprakkale, built by the Crusaders, marks the entrance to the Plain. A turning from the main road just before Iskenderun leads to Yakacik, where a complex of 16th century Ottoman buildings, including a mosque, covered bazaar and fortress can be seen. To the north of Iskenderun is Dortyol where one can visit the various monuments: the Cinkulesi (tower of the Jinns), a covered bazaar, Turkish baths, a fountain and a mosque.

On the coast to the south of Iskenderun is the little fishing port of Arsuz. Here there are beaches, hotels, guest houses and restaurants.

On the road to Antakya, after crossing the Belen Pass, it is possible to make a detour to the castle of Bagras, which was one of the principal strongholds of the Frankish principality of Antioch.

ANTAKYA

Pleasantly situated in a fertile plain, surrounded by grand mountains is Antakya, the ancient Antioch on the Orontes. Antakya was the prosperous and ostentatious capital of the Seleucid kings and was notorious for its luxurious life and pleasures. In Roman times the city was a great centre of artistic, scientific and commercial activities. It was also a centre of Christianity, and St. Barnabus, St. Paul and St. Peter stayed there at various times. From the end of the 11th century for 200 years, it was a Frankish principality held by the Crusaders.

Points of interest in the city include a picturesque bazaar and the mosque of Habib Neccar. Of particular interest is the Hatay Museum which houses one of the richest collections of Roman mosaics in the world, all of which were discovered in the environs of Antakya. A little outside the town is the Grotto of St. Peter, the cave church from which St. Peter preached for the first time and founded the Christian community. The holiness of the site was declared by the Vatican in 1983.

In the environs of Antakya are numerous places to visit: to the south is Harbiye, the gardens and waterfalls of Daphne, the city of pleasures; the Castle of Antioch from which a magnificent view of the city, plain and sea can be seen; and the site of the ancient Seleucia of Pieria next to the vast beach of Samandag.

CENTRAL ANATOLIA

The tawny-yellow central Anatolian plateau, slashed by ravines and dotted with volcanic peaks, forms the heartland of Turkey.

It has been the homeland of many peoples and the historic battleground of East and West. Here the Hattis, Hittites, Phrygians, Galatians, Romans, Byzantines, Seljuks and Ottomans established their rule. In its turbulent history the plateau has seen such invaders as Alexander the Great and Tamerlane march by. In ten millenia of their art, the people of the plateau have reflected the dramatic contours of the surrounding landscape, from the vigorous paintings of Catalhoyuk to the bold lines of Seljuk Turkish architecture right down to the impressive form of Ataturk's mausoleum.

ANKARA

Turkey's capital city is set in the strategic heartland of Central Anatolia, a site chosen by the founder of the modern Turkish Republic, Mustafa Kemal Ataturk. Though the city is modern in appearance, its origins date back to a hittite settlement in the 2nd millenium BC. In the 10th century BC the Phrygians established the city of Ancyra on the side, and seven centuries later the Galatians made Ancyra their capital. However it was not until after the First World War that Ankara leapt into the forefront of history as the centre of the national resistance led by Ataturk, which liberated the Turkish homeland from foreign powers. On 13th October, 1923, Ankara was declared the capital of the new independent Turkey.

HOW TO GET THERE
THY has regular flights has regular flights to Ankara. International airline flights are less frequent, but there are THY connecting flights from Istanbul.

The E-5 highway passes through Ankara, as does the railway connecting Ankara to Istanbul in the west.

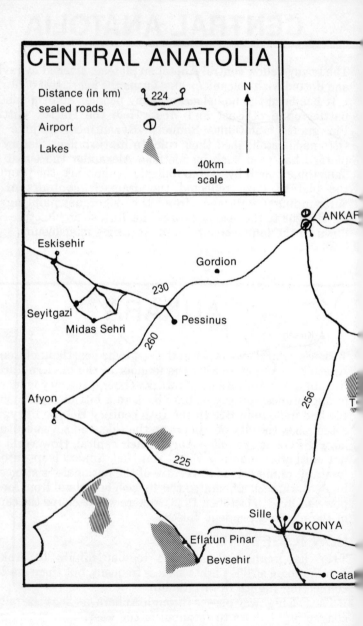

CENTRAL ANATOLIA

Distance (in km)
sealed roads   224

Airport   ⊕

Lakes

N

40km
scale

Eskisehir

Gordion

ANKAF

Seyitgazi

Midas Sehri

Pessinus

230

260

256

T

Afyon

225

Sille

⊕KONYA

Eflatun Pinar

Beysehir

Cata

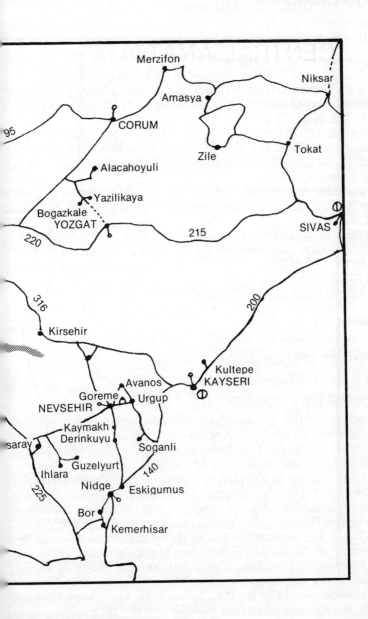

ACCOMMODATION–ANKARA

(Accommodation for other cities and towns in Central Anatolia is listed at the end of this chapter.)

A few names and addresses:
Buyuk Ankara (HL), Ataturk Bul. 183, Tel. 34 49 20-40.
Ankara Dedeman (H1), Buklum Sok. 1, Tel. 13 91 90-95; Buyuk Surmeli (H1), Cihan Sok 4, Tel.30 52 40; Kent (H1), Ataturk Bul. 195, Tel. 31 21 11-8.
Altinisik (H2), Necatibey Cad, 46. Tel. 291185-90; Bulvar Palas (H2), Ataturk Bul. 141, Tel. 342180-89; Etap Mola (H2), Ataturk Bul. 80, Tel. 339065 (US$50 ppn); Stad (H2), Istiklal Cad. 20 ulus, Tel. 12 42 20.
Ersan (H3), Mesrutiyet Cad. 13, Tel. 18 98 75; Guleryuz (H3), Sanayi Cad. 37, Tel. 124120-2; Sultan (H3), Bayindir Sok. 35, Tel. 315980-3.
Akman (H4), Itfaiye Meydani Tavus Sok 6, Tel. 24 41 40; Gulpalas (H4), Bayindir Sok 15, Tel. 33 31 20 (US$10 ppn); Safir (H4), Denizciler Cad. 34, Tel. 241194; Tac (H4), Cankiri Cad 35, Tel. 24 31 95.
Motel–Golbasi Angora Turistik Tesisleri, Tel. 137 537 38
Camping–Altinok Mocam, Ankara-Istanbul road 22 km from Ankara, Tel. 43 13 66
Cumhuriyet Youth Hostel–Cebeci/Ankara, Tel. 19 36 34

TOURIST INFORMATION OFFICE

Gazi Mustafa Kemal Bul. 33, Tel. 29 29 30-95

POINTS OF INTEREST

Dominating the modern part of the city is the limestone Mausoleum of Ataturk (Arnikabir). Completed in 1953, this mixture of classical and modern architectural concepts is undoubtedly the chief work of modern Turkish architecture. Ataturk's house is situated in Cankaya, near the Presidential Palace, and is now a museum. The oldest parts of the city are in and around the medieval citadel. Inside the walls is the Seljuk Alaeddin Mosque (12th century). Close to the gate of Hisar Kapisr is the restored Bedesien (covered bazaar) housing the Museum of Anatolian Civilisations and its priceless collection of Paleolithic, Neolithic, Hatti, Hittite and Phrygisn works. (Open every day except Monday.)

Outside the citadel are the 13th century Arslanhane Mosque, the 14th century Ahi Elvan Mosque and the 16th century Yeni

Cami (New Mosque). Beneath the citadel, around Ulus Meydani (Nation Square) are such Roman remains as the baths, the Column of Justinian and the Temple of Augustus, beside the 15th century Haci Bayram Mosque. From Ulus Meydani, with its equestrian statue of Ataturk, you can continue down Ataturk Boulevard, on which is the Ethnnographical Museum. Nearby is the Museum of Fine Arts.

DISTRICT ATTRACTIONS

ESKISEHIR (232km from Ankara). Eskisehir was founded in the 1st millenium BC by the Phrygians. Running through the city is the River Porsuk, and of interest is the 13th century Alaeddin Mosque, and the 16th century Kursunju Mosque. Just 41 km. to the south of the city are the Ottoman buildings of Sevitgazi.

GORDION (94km from Ankara on the Eskisehir road, right turn for Yassihoyuk, 12km) was the Phrygian capital and the place where Alexander the Great cut the Gordion Knot that gave him the key to Asia. At the site is the great earth tumulus of King Midas, famed in the legends of the 'Golden Touch' and the 'Asses Ears'. Also the foundations of the ancient city can be seen.

PESSINUS (133km from Ankara on the Eskisehir road, left turn 13km) was a Phrygian cult centre, and among the ruins is the Temple of Cybele, the mother goddess.

MIDAS SEHRI (66km south of Eskisehir past Seyilgazi) has an open air cult temple, inscriptions and ruins.

CANKIRI (131km from Ankara). Under the Galatians in the 3rd century BC the settlement was called Gangrea, and then it was called Kanon right down to Ottoman times. Above the city are the ruins of an 11th century fortress and in the city is the Ulu Cami (Great Mosque) built by Turkey's greatest architect, Sinan, in the 16th century. Just outside the city is the Ilgaz National Park and Ski Centre.

CORUM (242km from Ankara). It was after the Turkish conquest that the city took its name in the 11th century. Of interest is the 13th century Ulu Cami (Great Mosque) and the 19th century Ulu Cami (Great Mosque with tower).

BOGAZKALE (180km from Ankara on the Samsun road, turn right 22km). The Hittite capital of Hattusas is ringed with double walls broken by a Royal Gate, the Lion Gate and the Yer

Kapi (an underground tunnel). The largest ruins on the site are those of the Great Temple of the Sorm God Tesup, surrounded by 70 storerooms. In 1180 BC Hattusas was devastated by the Phrygians. The city walls are being extensively restored. The Acropolis of Hattusas contains the government buildings, Imperial Palace and archives of the Hittite Empire.

YAZILIKAYA (2km from Bogazkale). This open-air pantheon contains fine reliefs of Hittite gods and kings dating from the 13th century BC.

ALACAHOYUK (36km from Bogazkale). Before the arrival of the Hittites, the site was the centre of the flourishing Hattian Bronze Age culture, and it was from the royal tombs of this period that the gold and bronze objects in Ankara's Museum of Anatolian Civilisations were uncovered. All the standing remains, like the Sphinx Gate, date from Hittite times.

YOZGAT (217lm from Ankara). The city was founded in the 18th century under the Ottomans. Dating from this period is the Capanoglu Mosque and the adjoining Suleyman Sey Mosque. The 19th century Nizamoglu Konagi is an important work of Turkish architecture which now houses ethnographical exhibits. 5km south of Yozgat is the Camlik National Park.

AMASYA (336km from Ankara). Set in a narrow gorge of the Yesilirmak river, Amasya dates from the 3rd century BC. On the craggy rock face of the gorge are the ruins of the citadel, inside which are the remains of an Ottoman palace and an underground passageway. Hewn from the rock face above the city, are the impressive Roman rock tombs. Among the city's many historical buildings are the 13th century Seljuk Burmali Minare Mosque, the 15th century Yildirim Beyazit Mosque, the 15th century Beyazit Medresse, a theological school with reliefs, the Turumtay Turbesi (mausoleum) and the Gok Medresse, now a museum containing the mummies of the Mongol Ilhanid rulers of Amasya.

MERZIFON (50km north west of Amasya). Of interest in the town are several Ottoman monuments such as Celebi Sultan Mehmet Medresse and the Kara Mustafa Pasa Mosque.

TOKAT (422 km. from Ankara). The Tokat region is an important centre of Turkish culture. Among the city's main historical buildings are the ruins of the 28 tower castle, the 12th century Garipler Mosque, the 16th centure Ali Pasa Mosque and the 17th century Ulu Cami (Great Mosque). The Pervane Bay Darussifasi (or Gok Medresse), one of Tokat's finest buildings, is now a museum. Spanning the Yelisirmak is a 12th century Seljuk bridge.

NIKSAR (69km north east of Tokat), one-time capital of the Turkish Danismend Emirs, has a well preserved citadel, the 12th century Yagbasan Medresse and the Ulu Cami (Great Mosque), some of the oldest Turkish monuments in Turkey.

ZILE (67km west of Tokat). It was here that Julius Caeser pronounced the words 'Veni, vidi, vidi' (I came, I saw, I conquered). Beneath the fortress is the restored Ulu Cami (Great Mosque) of 1269.

SIVAS (441km from Ankara). Sivas was an important commercial centre on the crossroads of the Persia and Baghdad caravan routes. From 1142 to 1171 it was the capital of the Turkish Danismend Emirs. In 1919 the National Congress that took the decision to liberate Turkey from occupying powers, was held in Sivas. Of the many historical buildings there are the Danismend Ulu Cami (Great Mosque), the 13th century Izzeddin Keykavus Sifahanesi and the beautifully decorated Gok Medresse, the Cifte Minare Medresse and the Buruciye Medresse, all of 1271.

DIVRIGI (174km south-east of Sivas) was a Byzantine site that became the capital of the Turkish Mengucek Emirs in the 12th and 13th centuries. Above the town is a ruined citadel, and beneath this is the Ulu Cami (Great Mosque) completed in 1229.

KAYSERI (314km from Ankara). Kayseri, the Roman Caeserea and the capital of the province of Cappadocia, lies at the foot of the extinct volcano Erciyes Dagi (3916m) which is today a ski centre. Close to the Byzantine fortress is the Huand Mosque and Medresse, and the Mahperi Hatun Turbesi, a complex erected in the 13th century by the wife of the Seljuk Sultan Alaeddin Keykubat, the Princess Mahperi. Further to the south of the complex is the beautifully decorated Doner Kumbet of 1276, the Archeological Museum and the Kosk Medresse, a Mongol building of classical simplicity. Close to the city's bedesten (covered bazaar) is the restored Ulu Cami, originally built in the 12th century. Of Kayseri's many medresses the Cifte Medresse is the most interesting, since it was the first medieval school of anatomy.

KULTEPE (21km beyond Kayseri on the Sivas road, left turn 2km) was the site of the Hittite city of Kanesh, though only the foundations can be seen. Many finds from this site can now be seen in Kayseri's Archeological Museum.

SULTAN HAN (46km beyond Kayseri on the Sivas road). This caravanserai, built by the Seljuk Sultan Alaeddin Keykubat in the early 13th century, is one of the most beautiful in Anatolia.

50km south of Kayseri are the Sultan Marshes which are of interest for ornithologists.

KIRSEHIR (181km from Ankara). Founded in ancient times, Kirsehir became in the middle ages, the centre of the Ahi Brotherhood, a moslem sect based on moral and social ideals, that played an important role in the spiritual and political life of Anatolian towns. Among Kirsehir's many fine Seljuk buildings are the Cacabey Mosque of 1272 (a former astronomical observatory), the Alaeddin Mosque of 1230 and the Ahi Evran Mosque, beside which is the turbe (mausoleum) of the founder of the Ahi sect. On the Kayseri road out of Kirsehir is the Asik Pasa Turbesi of 1333, built during the period of Mongol rule.

NEVSEHIR (274km from Ankara). The city, the largest in the region of Cappadocia, developed greatly in the 18th century under the Grand Vizier Ibrahim Pasa. Dating from this period is the Kursunlu Mosque, and from the Seljuk period there is the Kaya Mosque.

URGUP (19km east of Nevsehir). At the foot of a cliff riddled with troglodyte dwellings, Urgup, together with Nevsehir is the main tourist accommodation centre of the region.

GOREME Open-Air Museum (8km north-west of Urgup). This monastic complex of rock churches and chapels covered with frescoes is one of the best known sites of Central Anatolia. The frescoes vary a little in date, the simplest and most geometric being from the late 8th or 9th centuries, and the more elaborate from the 10th to 13th centuries. Visit here the tiny Elmali Kilise (the Church with the Apple) which is decorated with scenes from the life of Christ and the saints and prophets. In the Yilani Kilise (the Church with the Snake), the Emperor Constantine and St. Helen are shown in the frescoes. The Barbara Kilise (the Church of St. Barbara) has many fine frescoes, as has the Karanlik Kilise (the Dark Church).

Kusadasi Harbour

Bodrum

Marmaris

Nearby is the Carikli Kilise (the Church with Sandals), so called from the footprints painted under the Ascension. On the road to Goreme there is the largest and most interesting of the churches in this area, the Tokatli Kilise (the Church with the Buckle). The paintings on the arch of the narthex and the walls of the nave date from the 13th century. They show the life of Christ from the Annunciation to the Ascension with great liveliness and detail. Among the many saints depicted here are St. Basil, a native of this area and Bishop of Caeserea (Kayseri), and St. George, traditionally associated with Cappadocia.

The frescoes of the churches in this region are currently under restoration by the joint efforts of the Ministry of Culture and Tourism and UNESCO.

CAVUSIN, ZELVE, AVANOS: On the road leading north from Goreme are the troglodyte town of Goreme with its houses attached to rock cones, Cavusin, with its churches in a rock face, the red-coned monastic complex of Zelve and finally Avanos, with its old houses, famous for its pottery and onyx.

The Ozkonak Underground City, 21km north of Avanos is the largest underground city in the region.

UCHISAR and ORTAHISAR: On the road from Avanos back to Nevsehir is the village of Uchisar, clustered around a rock pinnacle, from which there is a splendid view of the whole erosion basin. Off the Nevsehir-Urgup road is Ortahisar, another village at the foot of a crag honeycombed with caves.

SOGANLI (63km south-east of Nevsehir). In the valley are around sixty chapels, some of which have had the natural rock cones above them carved into domes.

KAYMAKLI and DERINKUYU (19 and 29km south of Nevsehir) were intriguing underground cities of rooms interconnected by tunnels, used in Byzantine times as refuges from raids.

HACIBEKTAS (46km north of Nevsehir). In the town is the beautifully preserved seminary of the Bedtasi order of dervishes and the turbe (mausoleum) of the order's founder, the 13th century mystic Haci Bektas Veli.

On Kizkalesi Island opposite the Kubad-Abad Saray is a Seljuk palace.

NIGDE (341km from Ankara). The 'Nahita' of ancient times,

Nigde is situated in a valley flanked by volcanic peaks, commanding an ancient trade route from Anatolia to the Mediterranean. Nigde's castle owes its present form to the Seljuks, and from the same period is the elegant Alaeddin Mosque. Dating from the 14th century period of Mongol rule are the Sungur Bey Mosque and the Hudavend Hatun Turbesi, one of the finest mausolea in Anatolia. The 15th century Ak Medresse is now an Archaeological Museum.

ESKIGUMUS (9km along the Nigde-Kayseri road, right turn 5km). The Byzantine monastery and church with their fresco covered walls, amongst the best preserved in Anatolia, date from the 10th and 11th centuries.

BOR (14km south of Nigde) was a former Hittite settlement and its historical buildings include the Seljuk Alaeddin Mosque and an Ottoman bedesten.

KEMERHISAR (5km south of Bor) was the site of the important Roman city of Tyana.

AKSARAY (120km north-west of Nigde). Though important in Seljuk times, most of Aksaray's historical buildings date from the 15th century, such as the Ulu Cami and the Zinciriye Medresse. Just 40km to the west of the town is the well preserved caravanserai of Sultan Han, built by the Seljuk Sultan Alaeddin Kaykubat.

IHLARA (11km from Aksaray on the Nevsehir road, right turn 32km). Here the Melendiz River has eroded a canyon into which Byzantine rock chapels covered with frescoes have been cut. Some of the best known are the Agacalti Kilisesi, also known as the Daniel Church, the Yilanli Kilise, the Hyacynth Church.

GUZELYURT (25km from Ihlara) is another interesting valley with dwellings dating from prehistoric periods. There are rock carved churches, chapels and a rock carved mosque.

KONYA (263km from Ankara). In the heart of the Anatolian plateau lies the city of Konya, famous for its Seljuk architecture and for its connection with the great mystic Mevlana, founder of the Order of the Whirling Dervishes.

Konya is a very ancient city. According to Phrygian legend it was the first city to emerge after the Flood. There was a prehistoric and later a Hittite settlement here, but the first important town was founded by the Phrygians. In Roman times as Iconium, it was already an important centre of trade. St. Paul and St. Barnabas both stayed in Konya on several occasions and preached there.

But Konya is known above all as the capital of the Seljuk rulers from the 11th to the 13th centuries. During the first half of the 13th century Konya reached the peak of its prosperity and cultural importance during the reigns of Sultan Alaeddin Keykubat and his successors. During this period most of the mosques, medresses, mausoleums and palaces were built. It was in these years too, that the renowned mystic philospher Celaleddin Rumi, known as Mevlana, settled in Konya and began teaching his disciples.

The ceremony of the 'Sema' takes place every year in Konya in the month of December to commemorate the death of Mevlana.

The most famous building in Konya is the Mevlana Mausoleum, the old monastery where the Order of Dervishes was founded. Dominated by a conical turquoise-blue tiled dome, the complex today houses a museum–open every day except Monday. Of special interest are the earliest manuscripts of Mevlana's great mystic epic poem, the 'Mesnevi', and some of the few surviving illuminated Seljuk manuscripts, as well as early musical instruments, dervish clothes and fine prayer rugs.

The Alaeddin Mosque, completed during the reign of Alaeddin Keykubat, is in the centre of the city. The mimber (pulpit) and mihrab (altar) are masterpieces of woodcarving. Adjoining the mosque are the mausoleums of many Seljuk Sultans. Just beside the Alaeddin Mosque are the remains of a wall of a Seljuk Palace.

Opposite the mosque is the Karatay medresse, which was built in the 13th century and has a marble portal; it now houses the Museum of Ceramics (open every day except Monday) with displays of rare Seljuk ceramics.

Beside the Alaeddin Park is the Ince Minareli medresse, with a portal decorated with geometric designs interlaced with intricate natural motifs all carved on stone. The building is now a museum of stone and wood carvings, including many fine Seljuk reliefs and statues.

The Archeological Museum displays many pieces from ancient Iconium and surroundings, notably a sarcophagus from the 3rd century BC with a bas relief showing the twelve tasks of Hercules. The Koyunoglu Museum houses archeological finds and has ethnographical displays. The lively bazaar is a good place to buy carpets, especially famous in Konya for their colours and quality. After a walk through the bazaar stop for the Konya Tandir Kebab speciality. For a relaxing cup of tea or a meal there are cafes and restaurants in the Fair Grounds or Meram (8km) on a hill that overlooks the city.

CATALHOYUK (45km south of Konya). This fascinating neolithic site dating back to the 8th millenium BC is one of the world's oldest towns where the mud houses were entered through holes in the roofs. The famous temple and mother goddess cult figures and neolithic frescoes from the site are now displayed in Ankara's Museum of Anatolian Civilisations.

IVRIS (168km from Konya). Here is a large bas relief of a king and fertility god, one of the finest.

SILLE (10km north of Konya) has a Byzantine church and several rock chapels with frescoes.

BEYSEHIR (94km west of Konya). This was an important Seljuk centre. Of interest are the Seljuk Esrefoglu Mosque and Mausoleum and the Kubad Abad Seljuk Summer Palace, 30km south-west on the lake shore. Situated in the lake is the Kiz Kalesi Island and Seljuk Palace. Do not miss a tasty fish dinner at one of the restaurants in Beysehir.

EFLATUN PINAR (114km west of Konya) has an unusual Hittite monumental fountain.

KARAMAN (110km south of Konya). This town was formerly the capital of the Karamanid Emirate, the first Turkish state to use Turkish as the official language as opposed to Persian. Also in the town is the burial place of Yunus Emre, the first great Turkish poet of the 13th century to write in Turkish. The castles date from Seljuk times and among the many Karamanid buildings are the Araboglu, Yunnus Emre and Aktekke Mosques and the Hatuniye Medresse. There is an Archeological Museum here.

ALAHAN (50km south of Karaman) has the quite well-preserved remains of a Byzantine monastery.

AKSEHIR (130km nothe-west of Konya). This town is well known as the birthplace of the 13th century humorist Nasrettin Hoca, whose mausoleum can be seen in the town. Also of interest are the 13th century Ulu Cami and the Altinkale Mescidi. The Tas Medresse is now the archeological museum.

ACCOMMODATION–CENTRAL ANATOLIA

Hotels–
Amasya–Turban Amasya (H3), Helkis Mah, Tel. 3134; Suluova–Saracogiu Muzaffer Tur. Tes. (H3), Amasya-Samsun Karayolu, Tel. 10-783.

Cankiri–Sehir (H4), Kastamonu Cad. 1/A, Tel. 1388.

Corum–Turban Corum (H3), Cepri Mah, Tel. 5311-13; Kolagasi (H4), Inonu Cad. 97, Tel. 1971-2930.

Eskisehir–Buyuk (H3), 27 Mayis Cad. 40, Tel. 12162-11248; Has Termal (H3), Hamam Yolu Cad. 7, Tel. 17819-19191; Porsuk (H3), Yunus Emra Cad. 103, Tel. 15005; Sultan Temel (H3), Hamam Yolu Cad. 1, Tel. 183371; Dural (H4), Yunus Emre Cad, 97, Tel. 11347-13521; Sale (H4), Inonu Cad. 17/1, Tel. 14743-14144.

Kayseri–Turan (H2), Turan Cad. 8, Tel. 11968-12506; Hattat (H3), Istanbul Cad. 1, Tel. 19331-19829; Terminal (H4), Istanbul Cad. 76, Tel. 15846.

Konya–Basak Palas (H3), Hukumet Me, y, 3, Tel. 11338-39; Ozkaymak Park (H3), Otogar Karsisi, Tel. 33770; Sahin (H3), Hukumet Alani 6, Tel. 13350-12376; Yeni Sema (H3), Yeni Meram Yolu, Tel. 13279-15992; Dergah (H4), Mevlana Cad 19, Tel. 11197-17661; Sema 11 (H4), Otogar Yani, Tel. 32557-30138; Selcuk (H4), Aleaddin Cad. Babalik Sok, Tel. 11259-14161.

Nevsehir–Goreme (H2), Hukumet Cad.16, Tel. 1706-07; Orsan Kapadokya (H3), Kayseri Cad. Tel. 1035-2115; Lale (H4), Gazhane Sok, Tel. 1797-2905; Viva (H4) Kayseri Cad 45, Tel. 1326-1760..

Nigde–Merkez Turist (H3), Hukumet Mey, Tel. 1860.

Sivas–Kosk (H2), Ataturk Cad. 11, Tel. 1150-1473; Sultan (H4), Belediye Sok, Tel. 12986-14021..

Tokat–Plevne (H4), Gaziosmanpasa Bul. 71, Tel. 2207; Turist (H4), Cumhuriyet Mey, Tel. 1610.

Yozgat–Yilmaz (H4), Ankara Cad. 14, Tel. 1107-1361 (US$15 ppn).

Camping–
Nevsehir–Kervansaray Goreme Mocamp on the Nevsehir-Urgup road, 2km from Nevsehir, Tel. 1428; Koru Mocamp, Tel 2157,

Uchisar; Paris Camp on the Nevsehir-Urgup road, 6km from Urgup, Orthisar.

TOURIST INFORMATION OFFICES

Aksaray–Bankalar Cad. Belediye Ishani, kat. 1, Tel. 2474.
Nevsehir–Lale Cad. 22, Tel. 1137
Urgup–Kayseri Cad. 37, Tel. 59.

THE BLACK SEA COAST

The Black Sea Coast will astound those who think of Turkey as an arid desert. The mountain slopes are thick with pine forests and the beaches extend for miles. There are delightful hills and dales, fishing villages with timber houses, and the warm humid climate is just right for the cultivation of tea, tobacco, maize, and hazel nuts. This coast is one of the most outstanding regions of the whole country.

In the 7th century the area was settled by Miletian colonists, and later came under the successive domination of Alexander the Great, the Roman and the Byzantine empires. In 1461 it was brought into the Ottoman Empire by Sultan Mehmet 11, the Conqueror. From this rich past, fascinating remains may be seen on all sides.

HOW TO GET THERE

By Road-There is a road in good condition, apart from one stretch about 100km long, running between Inebolu and Sinop, which follows the coast. This road will take you to the area's little ports and villages.

By Boat-Turkish Maritime Lines runs a year round ferry-boat service between Istanbul-Samsun-Trabzom.

By Air-There are regular air connections from Ankara and Istanbul to Trabzon and Samsun.

ACCOMMODATION

Artvin
Hotels-Karahan (H3), Inonu Cad., Tel. 1800-3; Papilla (H3), Ortahopa Cad., Tel. 1440-41.

Bolu
Hotels-Yurdaer (H3), Belediye Mey, Tel. 2903-4-5; Menekse (H4), Hurriyet Cad. 1, Tel. 1522-1700
Motels-Cizmeci, Kilicasian Kovu, Tel. 1066-4789; Emniyet, Ayrilik Cesmesi Mev., Tel. 1290; Koru, Omerler Koyu Bakirli Mev., Tel. 2528.

Giresun
Hotel-Giresun (H4), Ataturk Bul. 7, Tel. 3017-2469

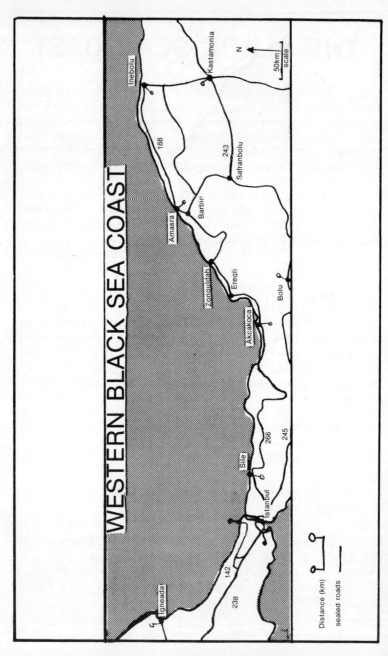

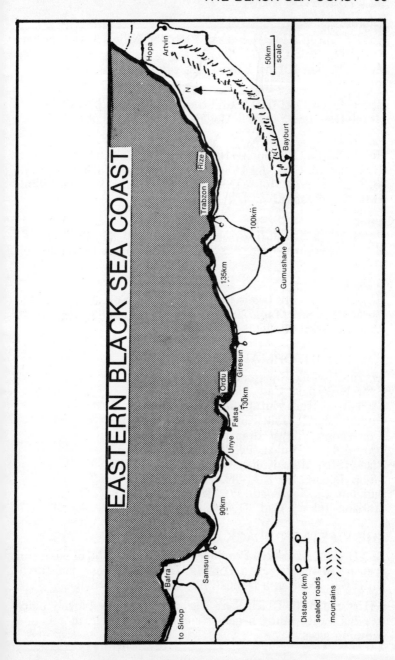

EASTERN BLACK SEA COAST

Hopa
Artvin
Rize
Trabzon
Bayburt
100km
135km
Gumushane
Giresun
Ordu
Fatsa
130km
Unye
90km
Bafra
Samsun
to Sinop

50km scale

N

Distance (km)
sealed roads
mountains

Kilyos
Hotels-Gurup (H4), Kale Cad. 21/1, Tel. Kilyos 1-194; Kilyos
Kale (H4), Kale Cad. 78, Tel. 54
Motel-Turban Kilyos, Kilyos, Tel. 142 02 88

Ordu
Hotel-Turist Otel (H3), Sahil Cad. 26, Tel. 114 66-142 73
Motel-Dolunay, Yaprakli Mevkii, Fatsa, Tel. 1528

Samsun
Hotels-Turban Samsun (H1), Ataturk Bul., Tel. 107 50-5; Yafeya
(H2), Genclik Cad., Tel 165 66-67; Burc (H4), Kazimpasa Cad.
36, Tel. 154 79-80; Gokce (H4), Sahil Cad., Tel. 179 52-54; Vidinli
(H4), Kazimpasa Cad. 4, Tel. 160 50-51

Sinop
Hotel-Melia Kasim (H2), Dr. Riza Nur Cad. 41, Tel. 163-286
Motel-Koskburnu Tur. Tes., Koskburnu Mevkii, Gerze, Tel.
81-503

Trabzon
Hotels-Usta (H3), Iskele Cad. Telgrafpane Sok. 3, Tel. 121 95;
Horon (H4), Sira Magazalar 125, Tel. 111 99-122 89; Ozgur (H4),
Ataturk Alani 29, Tel. 113 19-127 78

TOURIST INFORMATION OFFICES

Artvin-Il Halk Kutuphanesi, Tel. 1135
Bolu-Ismetpasa Cad., Tel. 3690-3632
Girseun-Il Halk Kutuphanesi, Tel. 1626
Gumushane-Il Halk Kutuphanesi, Tel. 3472
Kastamonu-Vilayet Binase, Tel. 2300-2912
Ordu-Vilayet Binasi, Tel. 17100/202
Rize-Muftu Mah. Kultur Sitesi kat: 4, Tel. 13980
Sinop-Iskele Mey. 2/A, Tel. 1996
Samsun-19 Mayis Bul. 2/1, Tel. 11228-10014
Trabzon-Taksim Cad. 31, Tel. 14659

THE WESTERN BLACK SEA COAST

IGNEADA: In Trakya Province there is every kind of beautiful
scenery in the Istranca Forests; Igneada is near the Turco-
Bulgarian frontier, a typical, pleasant fishing village.

KILYOS: On the Black Sea's European coast, is a lovely place
to relax on its sandy beaches, comfortable hotels, motels and
camping sites.

SILE: On the Anatolian shore, 71km from Istanbul, Sile is an alluring little village of long sandy beaches. The holiday makers from Istanbul enjoy a weekend outing, and evenings of entertainment in its restaurants and night clubs.

Extending right to the sea, the town is dominated by a hill on which stands the remains of a Genoese castle. Embroidered blouses and nightwear are made here from 'sile bezi'. In this neighbourhood a road runs from the Anatolian shore at Beykoz about 25km to Polonezkoy which is an ideal place for those who wish to relax and wind down.

To the east of this coast are the natural beauties of Kerpe, Kefken and Karaus, delightful little fishing villages with restaurants and the limpid waters and sandy beaches of the Black Sea.

BOLU: Inland, in the west of the area, Bolu is an important centre on the Ankara–Istanbul road. In the city, known as Claudiopolis in Roman times, is the 14th century Ulu Cami with hot springs nearby. South-west (55km) is Lake Abant, situated in lovely alpine surroundings at an altitude of 1500m. Here the scenery and the comfortable facilities encourage visitors to extend their stay.

Kartalkaya, in the Koroglu mountains, is a local ski-centre and resting-place. Along the road you may stop off for picnic at the popular spot of the Golcuk Lake. North of Bolu is found the breathtaking beauty spot of 'Yedi Goller' (seven lakes) National Park. Mengen is famous for its good cooks, and holds an annual Chef Festival in August featuring traditional specialities.

AKCAKOCA: 42km from Duzce, 240km from Istanbul, this is a holiday resort with a lovely, clean beach and comfortable guest houses and hotels. Near the town are the remains of a Genoese castle.

EREGLI: 40km to the east of Akcakoca, Eregli stands on a hill by the site of a ruined Byzantine castle.

ZONGULDAK: 67km east of Eregli, this is a major city and a centre of coal production. It is an important port of the Black Sea.

SAFRANBOLU: In the interior region, to the south-east of Zonguldak, some of the most beautiful examples of old Turkish architecture may be seen in the timber houses of Safranbolu. The 'Turkish Delight' made here has an especially refined quality.

BARTIN: 17km south-east of Amasra is this pretty town with timbered houses. The remains of a Roman road dating from the time of the Emperor Claudius can be seen. At nearby Inkum is a holiday village with sandy beaches, restaurants and guest houses in a particularly beautiful setting.

AMASRA: 81km east of Zonguldak, Amasra stands on a peninsula split by two inlets, and is a little fishing port, one of the high points of the beauty of the Black Sea. By the town, on a rocky promontory, rise the ramparts of the Byzantine citadel. There is also a Byzantine church, now called the Fatih Cami, and a necropolis from the Roman period. The archeological museum will be of interest to some.

East of Amasra is the typical fishing village of Cakraz with its excellent beach. The road from Cakraz eastwards is particularly scenic passing through the towns of Kurucasile, where Black Sea fishing boats are made, and Cide which has good hotels and a pleasant beach.

INEBOLU: A typical Black Sea town set in lush greenery with fine examples of traditional Turkish architecture. East of Inebolu (24km) is the town of Abana, a holiday centre.

KASTAMONU: Another regional centre situated amidst forests. Here you can see a 12th century Byzantine castle at the foot of a hill. The 13th century Atabey Cami should not be missed, nor the Ibni Neccar Cami. There are also two museums in the town. Nearby is Ev Kaya, a rock-tomb dating from the 6th century BC. In the village of Kasaba the Mahmut Bey Cami has some of the nicest wood carvings to be seen anywhere in Turkey.

On the Kastamonu-Cankili road in the Ilgaz Mountains is a national park and ski-resort.

THE EASTERN BLACK SEA COAST

SINOP: 436km north-east of Ankara is one of the most beautiful natural harbours of the Black Sea. It was the birthplace of the cynic philosopher Diogenes, who lived in the 3rd century BC. From this period date the town citadel and the foundations of a temple dedicated to Serapis, found in the grounds of the archeological museum. On display in the museum are some beautiful golden icons. The 13th century Alaeddin Cami and the Alaiye Medresse should be seen. The charming fisherman's wharf with its brightly coloured boats and fish restaurants is a delightful place to relax, wine and dine. The town is also known for its traditional nautical wood carvings and good crystal. Seaside hotels and holiday villages will encourage you to stay here. Gerze with its beach and fish restaurants may be worth a visit.

BAFRA: 188km east of Sinop, Bafra is famous for its tobacco, caviar and thermal springs. Here one may see a 13th century hamam (bath), and a mosque-mausoleum-medresse complex from the 15th century.

SAMSUN: 418km north-east of Ankara, 168km east of Sinop, Samsun is a modern industrial city, and at the same time a major port of the Black Sea area. The region's products are exported from here. In the city park you can see an extraordinarily effective equestrian statue of Ataturk, and it will be remembered that on May 19, 1919, Ataturk landed here to organise the defence of the country. Amongst the city's mosques are the 14th century Pazar Cami and the 19th century Buyuk Cami. Finds from Dundar Tepe and the ancient Amisos are displayed in the archeological museum.

UNYE: 89km east of Samsun, is the charming little port of Unye, where the purple of the rocks contrasts with the blue of the sky and the green of the hazel nut plantations. Here the 18th century town hall building is a truly extraordinary sight. Beyond Unye, 3km, is the beautiful beach of Camik.

FATSA: 20km from Unye is another one of the holiday towns. The 50km scenic road to Ordu is dotted with fish restaurants serving sea snails and the finest tea found anywhere.

ORDU: 77km east of Unye, Ordu stands at the foot of a verdant hill. It was from here that the survivors of Xonophon's Ten Thousand embarked. Specially remarkable are an 18th century church, and the pretty beach of Guzelyali, 2km from the city.

GIRESUN: 52km east of Ordu, Giresun was founded by the ruins of a Byzantine fortress. A panoramic view of the area from the fortress is a must for the tourist who stops in this city.

From here the Roman general Lucullus carried the first cherry trees to Europe. In the city there is an 18th century church. Outside the city is Giresun Adasi (Giresun Island) which is said to have once belonged to the Amazons, and where the remains of a temple can be seen.

Between Giresun and Trabzon, surrounded by wooded

mountains are the villages of Kesap, Tirebolu, Gorele, Vakfikebir and Akcaabat which are important in terms of history, climate and beauty.

TRABZON: 345km to the east of Samsun, Trabzon was founded in the 7th century BC by Miletian colonists. Later, Alexis Comnenos founded the Comnene Empire here which endured until 1461. The city then fell into the hands of the Ottomans. On entering the city, on a green hill descending to the sea, is a well-preserved Byzantine monument–the 13th century Aya Sofya church. The walls of this church are decorated with frescoes, some of the finest examples of Byzantine craftmanship. In the city there is also an old Byzantine church which has now been turned into a mosque called the Fatih Cami. The Yeni Cuma Cami and the Ottoman Gulbahar Hatun Cami can be seen as well. The higher part of the city, the old quarter, inside the still-extant fortifications, should be visited with its timber houses and dark narrow streets. The house that Ataturk stayed in has now been turned into a museum.

Along a very beautiful road, 45km from Trabzon, on the face of a steep cliff there stands the 14th century Sumela Monastery. In its corridors, hallways and chapels there are some outstanding 14th and 18th century frescoes. Hamsikoy, set amongst beautiful mountains in the Zigana Pass, is famous for its food and is a favourite stop for tourists.

GUMUSHANE: Founded on the main route from Trabzon to Iran, Gumushane was once of considerable importance, although this has now faded. Nevertheless you can still see historical mosques and bath-houses, and the old-style architecture of the houses, churches and tombs.

BAYBURT: Bayburt is along the ancient Silk Route travelled by Marco Polo, and the well known Turkish traveller, Evliya Celebi. Here the remains of a Byzantine castle can be seen.

RIZE: 75km from Trabzon, Rize is a typical Black Sea city built on the mountain slopes that are covered with tea plantations. Among the things to be seen in the city are the 16th century Islam Pasa Cami and the remains of a Genoese castle. South of Rize is Uzungol a lovely alpine lake surrounded by mountains.

Turning inland after Ardesen on the road leading east from Rize, you come to the beautiful little town of Camlihemsin. Nearby is the Firtina Vadisi (Valley of Storms) with Zirkale

Castle and bridges from Byzantine times. Ayder, not far away, has many hot springs.

HOPA: 89km to the east of Rize is Hopa, the last port before the Turco-Russian border. The 64km from here to Artvin is again full of mountain scenery along with the curious foot bridges across the Coruh River.

ARTVIN: The main city of the province, Artvin stands at the foot of a hill crowned by the ruins of a 16th century castle. Artvin has beautiful old Turkish houses, and a winding mountain road leads up to and beyond Artvin Castle, offering a spectacular view. There is a famous annual bullfighting festival here, and on the Coruh River, white water rafting for the adventurous.

EASTERN TURKEY

The eastern region of Turkey is a diverse land which differs profoundly from the rest of the country. The Toros Mountains in the south and the chain of the Black Sea Mountains in the north, encircle the Anatolian Plateau and meet to form a complex mountain range in the east.

HOW TO GET THERE

Three axis roads cross the region: the northern highway, which begins in Ankara and reaches the Turco-Iranian frontier via Sivas, Erzincan, Erzurum and Agri; the central highway, which extends as far as Van Lake via Kayseri, Malatya and Elazig; the southern highway, a prolongation of the coastal Mediterranean road, which crosses the High Mesopotamian Plain and follows the borders of Iraq and Syria.

There is a train service from Ankara to the Turco-Iranian frontier, but because it follows a meandering route this is a rather slow way to travel. A new fast train service is to be introduced.

ACCOMMODATION

Hotels

Agri/Dogubeyazit–Beyazit (H3), Emniyet Ca. 48, Tel. 139-159

Diyarbakir–Demit (H3), Izzet Pasa Cad. 8, Tel. 12315-17; Buyuk Diyarbakir (H3), Inonu Cad. 4, Tel. 12444; Turistik (H3), Ziya Gokalp Bul. 7, Tel. 12662-3; Asian (H4), Kibris Cad. 23, Tel. 13971-18574; Canturkler (H4), Gazi Cad. Suakar Sok. 7, Tel. 12059-12470; Derya (H4), Inonu Cad. 33, Tel. 14966; Sarac (H4), Izzet Pasa Cad. 16, Tel. 12365-13058.

Elazig–Buyuk Elazig (H3), Harput Cad. 9, Tel. 22001-2-3; Beritan (H3), Hurriyet Cad. 24, Tel. 14484; Erdem (H4), Istasyon Cad. 19, Tel. 12212-11242

Erzincan–Urartu (H2), Cumhuriyet Mey., Tel. 1561-2041.

Erzurum–Oral (H2), Terminal Cad. 3, Tel. 19740-5; Sefer (H3), Istasyon Cad., Tel. 13615; Efes (H3), Tahtacilar Cad. 36, Tel. 17081-82; Buyuk Erzurum (H3), Yenikapi Mah.; Buhara (H4),

Black Sea Region

Eurfa   Harran Quasi

Eastern Turkey

Mount Ararat

Mardin

Adiyaman, Mount Nemrut

Kazim Karabekir Cad., Tel. 15096-17696; Cinar (H4), Ayazpasa Cad. 18, Tel. 13580; Krai (H4), Erzincan Kapi 18, Tel. 11930-16973; Polat (H4), Kazim Karabekir Cad., Tel. 11623-24 (US$10 ppn); Seref (H4), Cumhuriyet Cad., Tel. 17330-19886.

Pasinter-Kale (H4), Kaplicalar Mah., Tel. 1532-1362.

Gaziantep-Kaleli (H2), Hurriyet Cad. Guzeice Sok. 50, Tel. 13417-12718; Buyuk (H4), Karagoz Cad. 26, Tel. 11075-15222; Mimar (H4), Hurriyet Cad. 24, Tel. 17992-93; Murat (H4), Inonu Cad. 53, Tel. 15276; Turk (H4), Hurriyet Cad. 27, Tel. 19460

Nizip-Belediye (H4), Ataturk Bul. 30, Tel. 684.

Kars-Temel Palas (H4), Pazar Cad. 4/A, Tel. 1376; Yilmaz (H4), Kucukkazimbey Cad. 114, Tel. 1074-2387.

Malatya-Kent (H4), Ataturk Cad. 151, Tel. 12175-12813; Sinan (H4), Ataturk Cad. 14, Tel. 12907 (US$10 ppn).

Siirt-Erdef (H4), Cumhuriyet Cad. 9, Tel. 1081-82.

Sanliurfa-Turban Urfa (H3), Koprubasi Yusufpasa Mah., Tel. 3520.

Van-Akdamar (H2), Kazimkarabekir Cad. 22, Tel. 3036-2908; Buyuk Asur (H3), Cumhuriyet Cad. 126, Tel. 3753; Tekin (H3), Kucukcami Civari, Tel. 3010-1366; Beskardes (H4), Cumhuriyet Cad. 34, Tel. 1116-7; Caldiran (H4), Sihke Cad. Yenicami Karsisi, Tel. 2718; Kent (H4), Isbankasi Arkasi, Tel. 2404-2519; Guzel Reis (H4), Irfan Bastug Cad., Tel. 2026.

TOURIST INFORMATION OFFICES

Adiyaman-Hukumet Konagi, Zemin Kat, Tel. 1008.
Diyarbakir-Lise Cad. 24/A, Tel. 12173-17840.
Gurbulak-Turkish-Iranian frontier post-Tel. 9.
Kars-Faikbey Cad., Inonu Karakolu Karsisi, Tel. 2724.

EXCURSIONS

FROM ERZINCAN TO DOGUBAYAZIT

ERZINCAN (689 km from Ankara)

The principal city of the province, situated on a fertile plain, was the scene of a famous battle in 1243 between the Seljuks and the Mongols. Many of the bronze objects in Ankara's Museum of Anatolian Civilisations came from around here.

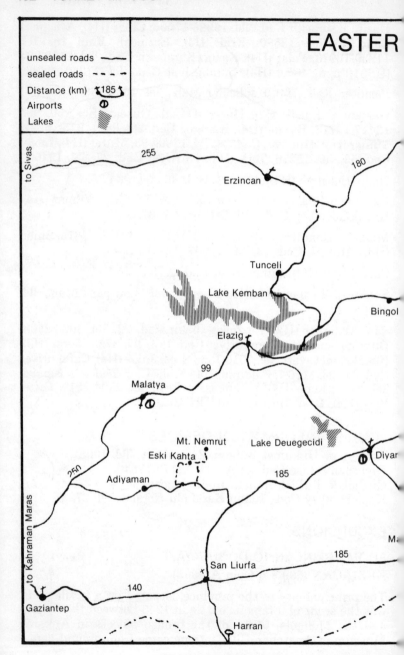

EASTER

unsealed roads ——
sealed roads ----
Distance (km) 185
Airports Φ
Lakes

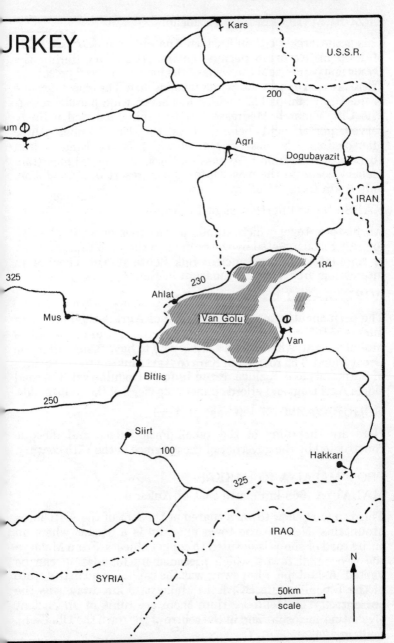

ERZURUM (193 km from Erzincan)

This is the largest city in Eastern Anatolia, and has an altitude of 1900 m. Erzurum became an important city during the Byzantine period, and the walls of the fortress are well preserved. There are also important Seljuk remains here. The oldest mosque is the Ulu Cami of 1179 which has seven wide parallel naves. The Cift Minareli Medresse has two minarets, and a finely carved portal, and behind it is the Uc Kumbet (three mausoleums), the best known of which is the Emir Sultan Turbesi. A road from here passing through splendid mountain scenery, leads to the new winter sports resort of Palandoken, only 6 km from Erzurum.

KARS (211 km north-east of Erzurum)

An historic town which stands at the foot of an impressive fortress reconstructed by the Seljuks in the 12th century. East of Kars (46 km) is the ancient Silk Route at Ani. There is an interesting archeological museum in Kars.

AGRI/ARARAT (226 km from Kars)

The permanently snow-covered peak of Agri is the highest in Turkey (5165 m). It is better known to the rest of the world as Mount Ararat, where Noah's ark is said to have rested after the Great Flood. The road from Kars to Agri runs via the ski-centre of Sarikamis and Tuzluca. From Igdir to Dogubayazit the road skirts Agri Dagi and affords panoramic views of the countryside.

DOGUBAYAZIT (95 km east of Agri)

Here are the ruins of the Ishak Pasa Palace and mosque constructed by the governor of the province in the 17th century.

FROM MALATYA TO HAKKARI

MALATYA (668 km south-east of Ankara)

This is a fairly new town, situated at the foot of the Anti-Toros Mountains. Next to the town museum is a bazaar where an entire road of shops is devoted to copper objects. From Malatya the two small towns which preceded its foundation can be visited: Aslantepe, 7 km away, was the capital of a Hittite state in the 1st millenium BC; Eski Malayta, 9 km away, was the ancient city of Melitene. Here there are ruins of an ancient Byzantine enclosure, and in the centre of the town the Ulu Cami, built in 1247.

ELAZIG (103 km. north-east of Malatya)

Another new city founded in the 19th century, standing at the foot of a mountain. There are several interesting mosques, and the mountain is crowned by a fortress of the ancient city of Harput, 5 km to the north. The huge artificial lake of Keban Dam is on the River Firat, 50 km from Elazig.

TUNCELI (136 km from Elazig)

The city of Tunceli lies on the Elazig-Ersurum road surrounded by mountains. The fortress of Pertek, which was constructed in the Middle Ages stands 31 km. along the road from Elazig. Nearby is the Munzur Valley National Park.

BINGOL (145 km from Elazig)

The name of the city means 'a thousand lakes' and there are, in fact, many glacier lakes in the surrounding mountains. In the city itself are the remains of a medieval fortress.

MUS (118 km east of Bingol)

This city was founded in the 6th century and the remains of a citadel, the Aslanhane Caravanserai, can be seen. There are also several mosques, such as the Ulu Cami and the Seljuk mosque of Alaeddin Pasa and Haci Seref.

BITLIS (85 km east of Mus)

Bitlis stands in the middle of a green oasis. There is a Byzantine citadel with polygonal towers overlooking the city, the Serefhan Medresse and several interesting mosques, the 12th century Ulu Cami, the Gokmeydani Mosque, built by the Seljuks, and the 16th century Serefiye Mosque. From nearby Tatvan there are boat and ferry connections across the lake to Van.

AHLAT (68 km north of Bitlis)

To the north of Lake Van, the largest lake in Turkey (at an altitude of 1720 m) are the ruins of the town of Ahlat. In the 12th century this city was the capital of the Moslem state that ruled the Van basin. Of interest are several mausoleums of the Seljuk period, notably Ulu Kumbet, the Bayindir Turbesi, the Hasan Pasa Kumbet and the Cifte Kumbet. There are also inscribed monumental tombstones from the 12th century. At Adilcevaz to the north of Ahlat there is an Ulu Cami on the lake shore, and the Urartian Temple of Haldi.

AKDAMAR (124 km from Bitlis, 41 km from Van)

On a small island in Lake Van stands the 10th century church of the Holy Cross with its outer walls richly decorated with Old Testament reliefs.

VAN (168 km from Bitlis)

Van, the ancient Urartian capital of Tuspa, is situated by the lake of the same name, at the foot of a rocky peak crowned by an imposing citadel. Steps carved in the rock lead to the Urartian fortress, and half way up there are cuneiform inscriptions paying homage to Xerxes. In the old city are numerous mosques and mausoleums of the Seljuk and Ottoman periods. In the new city is an archeological museum. At Cavustepe, 35 km from Van, is an important Urartian site with temples, a palace and inscriptions. In Hosap (60 km) is a 17th century castle.

HAKKARI (205 Km from Van)

The small city of Hakkari is situated at an altitude of 1700 m and is dominated by a medieval fortress and a fine medresse. The road to Hakkari passes through the Zap Valley and mountains which contain some beautiful scenery.

FROM GAZIANTEP TO MARDIN

GAZIANTEP (687 km from Ankara)

This city is quite modern in appearance, but it is actually of Hittite origin. It is the centre of pistachio nut cultivation in Turkey. In the city is a Seljuk fortress and a medresse, and an archeological museum. The artisans of Gaziantep specialise in copper.

KAHRAMAN MARAS (80 km north of Gaziantep)

This was once the capital of the Hittite state of Gurgum (12th century BC). Inside the citadel is an archeological museum displaying Hittite sculptures. The Ulu Cami and the Tas Medresse are of the 15th century.

SANLIURFA (144 km east of Gaziantep)

Situated in the plain of High Mesopotamia, Sanliurfa is one of the most ancient cities in history. In the 2nd millenium BC it was the capital of a Hurrite state. It is traditionally believed that Abraham stayed here. Of interest are the remains of a crusader castle, at the foot of which stands the Halil Rahman mosque, next to a pool of sacred carp. On the other side of the pool is the Ottoman period Rizvaniye mosque of the 17th century.

HARRAN (49 km south of Sanliurfa on the Akcakale Road)

The village with its curious domed dwellings is believed to be the ancient city of Charan mentioned in the Book of Genesis, where Abraham spent several years of his life. There are a few remains at Harran, including those of the biggest ancient Islamic university, and the temple of Sin the Moon-God.

DIYARBAKIR (185 km north-east of Sanliurfa).

A lively city situated on a plateau close to the banks of the Dicle (Tigris). The triple black basalt walls than encircle the old town give it a medieval appearance. These ramparts, which have sixteen keeps and five gates, are among the longest in the world (5.5 km). They contain interesting inscriptions and reliefs. Notable for its original architecture, and the number of ancient materials used in its restoration, is the Ulu Cami. Nearby is the Mesudiye Medresse, which has an archeological museum.

MARDIN (96 km south of Diyarbakir)

Whereas Diyarbakir is a city of black appearance, Mardin is a city with a white aspect because of the limestone buildings. It stands on a hillslope and overlooks the vast Mesopotamian Plain. Of interest in the city are the ancient citadel and a few Islamic monuments. Only 7 km from Mardin, on the road to Akinci, lies the Jacobite monastery of Deyrulzaferan. At nearby Kiziltepe is one of the best examples of Seljuk architecture, the 13th century Ulu Cami with fine reliefs. At Midyat, east of Mardin is the ancient town famous for its silver objects known as Talkari. At Hasankeyf, on the road to Siirt are the ruins of a vast 12th century bridge that once spanned the Dicle (Tigris), a 13th century palace, and the 15th century Zeynei Bey Turbesi.

SIIRT (270 km from Mardin)

This principal city was important at the time of the Abbasid Caliphate. There are several interesting monuments including the 12th century Ulu Cami, the 13th century Asakir Carsi Cami. At Aydinlar, 6 km from Siirt, is the Ibrahim Hakki Mausoleum Complex. Nearby is the local Ibrahim Hakki astronomical museum.

ADIYAMAN

This area lies in the south-east of Turkey in the central Firat (Euphrates) region. According to archeological research the history of the area goes back to the Paleolithic Age. During the Neolithic Age (8000-7000BC) Gritille, Hayaz, Ancoz and Samsat were the main culture centres. After the Early Bronze Age the Hittites lived here and formed the Anatolian Federation. The region was populated successively by Mitanni, Urartians, Assyrians, Persians, Macedonians, the people of Commagene, Romans, Byzantines, Abbasidas, Omayyads, Seljuks, Ilkhaians, Mameluks and the Ottoman Empire.

HOW TO GET THERE

By air to Malatya, then road to Adiyaman.
By rail to Golbasi, then road.
By road-follow E24 to Gaziantep or Urfa.

ACCOMMODATION

Motels–Arsemia Moteli, Bahcelievler Mah. Nemrut Yolu Uzeri 146, Tel. 2112-3131; Nemrut Moteli, Girne Mah., Kahta, Tel. 459.

TOURIST INFORMATION OFFICE

Ataturk Blvd., 41, Tel. 1008.

EXCURSIONS

In the centre of Adiyaman are the remains of a fortress built by the Omayyad Caliph, Hisn-i Mansur, in the 8th century and later restored by the Seljuks. Today this fortress is a park. A mosque, Ulu Cami, from the 14th century is of importance.

A colourful place for shopping is the Oturakci Carsisi where you can buy local handicrafts, rugs, kilims and saddle bags. The ancient city of Perre, today called Pirin, is 5km from Adiyaman. The city ruins and 208 caves in the rocks, where there are human reliefs, are of historical importance. At the Adiyaman Museum you will find on display archeological and ethnographical artefacts rom various historical periods. The museum is open every day except Monday.

OUTLYING ATTRACTIONS

NEMRUT DAGI (Mt. Nemrut) is the first impressive peak rising from a flat plain in Northern Mesopotamia and it rises to a height of 2150m. It is matchless in its historical treasures. The original peak was removed and in its place was constructed the Tumulus of Antiochos 1, one of the kings of Commagene when it was at its height of power and art expression during the 1st century BC. This interesting structure was made by heaping up pieces of rocks to make the 50m x 150m mound. The east and west terraces of this mound are open-air temples. On these terraces are statues of lions, eagles, five gigantic god statues, four male and one female.

Dexiosis type reliefs are in a good state of preservation. On the western terrace the heads of these statues have been toppled but are in good condition. The heads alone are taller than a man. On the eastern terrace the 9m high statues are well enough preserved to see the gods sitting on their thrones. The statues are in the same order on both terraces; Apollo, Tyche–the Commagene god of fertility, Zeus, Antiochus and Hercules. Reliefs of the geneology of Antiochus as well as others are now being restored. Opposite, at the other end of the terrace, is an altar with several steps leading up to it from all four sides.

In order to reach Nemrut Dagi, which is 83km from Adiyaman and 48km from Kahta, you proceed by minibus or taxi through Narince and Karadut up to 1km from the top. Here there is a rest area. Walk along a path from the rest area for 20 minutes and you reach the tumulus. The view is spectacular, and it is worth the climb to view the sunrise or sunset. To be enveloped by this natural beauty and live in history will leave one with an impression for a lifetime. May-October is the best time to visit the region.

ESKI KALE is near Eski Kahta (Kocahisar) and is the ancient fortress of Arsameia, built with no small effort on a steep cliff. Its walls and parapets are still in good condition. On a special path, that was used for religious ceremonies leading up the mountain side, is a statue pointing the direction to the temple. Another 100m further along is a Dexiosis relief showing a hand-shaking scene between King Mithradates and Hercules, carved in about 50BC. Near this relief are rooms hollowed into the rock that were used for religious ceremonies. Following along this footpath still upward you come to the largest rock inscription in Anatolia. It tells of the political intentions and the religious beliefs of the Commagene Kingdom, that Arsameia was its capital, and that Mithridates, the father of Antioches I, was buried there. Just below this inscription is a large opening that descends by a stone stairway to a depth of 158m. This passageway leads to Arsameia but now it is blocked off half-way along. Above this inscription, following the path up the mountain side, are the foundations and mosaic floors of the Arsameia Palace .

YENI KALE is the second fortress, and is located in the village of Kocahisar just opposite Eski Kale. The Kahta River runs between the two. This fortress is built on a 300-350m high rock. Archeologists have proven it to be the fortress for the kings of Commagene. Certain additions were made in Mameluk times to give the appearance it has today. The castle is surrounded by high walls with only one entrance gate. Inside are houses, shopping areas, a bazaar, a mosque, cisterns, a gaol and a dungeon.

CENDERE BRIDGE is a surviving Roman bridge built in the time of Septimus Severus. It spans the Kahta River in one single arch, and is constructed of 92 stones each weighing about 10 tons. The three columns, two at one end and one at the other, are 9-10m in height.

KARAKUS TUMULUS is 35m high and is the funeral monument of the Commagene royal families. The tumulus is surrounded by four 9-10m high columns which are surmounted by large animal figures.

INDEX